It's Right There

P.S.R. Ureh

For permission requests, write to the publisher at the address below:
P.S.R. Ureh
PSRUreh@PSRUreh.com
www.psrureh.com

Disclaimer:
The information contained in this manuscript is for general informational purposes only. The author and the publisher make no representations or warranties of any kind, express or implied, about the completeness, accuracy, reliability, suitability, or availability with respect to the contents of the manuscript for any purpose.
The author and the publisher disclaim any liability for any loss or damage arising from the use of information contained in this manuscript. Readers are advised to consult appropriate professionals for specific advice tailored to their situation and follow the laws applicable to them. The views expressed in this manuscript are solely those of the author and do not necessarily reflect the views of the publisher.

ISBN: 979-8-9899269-1-6

Published by P.S.R. Ureh LLC

Charlotte, North Carolina, 28262

Acknowledgments

I would like to thank all the individuals who gave me 3 minutes of their time to read Chapter 1 during the writing phase. The readings were a part of an experiment on how effective the book material can be when it's combined with my delivery. My hypothesis was correct, based on that data. Therefore, it was well needed as a grand reminder on the type of impact that "It's Right There" will have on the masses.

I appreciate Ana Carolina Scott for her well-rounded feedback during the first stage of the manuscript. The one Zoom call we had was very productive, and she suggested that I should include multiple Subchapters throughout the book.

Bryan Roberts is another person that gave effective feedback, including to use specific sources to cite.

Fatima Hassan deserves high praise also. Her editing made this book more of a masterpiece. She was very communicative and understood my vision.

I must give huge thanks to Jennifer Myers. Jennifer was key from the very start of the project. She's not just a writer; she's also family. Her wisdom, commitment to her family, and her acts of service is magnificent at the highest level. She's an Unstoppable Force!

Let's not forget my friend Maisha Sheldon for being the most consistent person that I have ever met in such a small-time frame. She was a huge part before publishing. Her early review and grammar checks was completely spectacular. A life saver! The exclusive early reading was completed by her in less than a week, and that says a lot when considering all the responsibilities she has towards her family. Not all heroes wear capes indeed.

Speaking of capes, Maria Bianka Mercedez Cureton is the only person that has stuck around for all these years. I'm giving her the utmost respect because she always knew who I was from the very start, and she waited for me to become the man that I am today. I know that I can count on her to be a part of the Unstoppable Force that leads the world to a better future.

I'm thankful for her, and so thankful for the time I had to complete the writing of this piece. Living in the United States, gave me so much data. This country is the most important country in this world for many reasons. It is the sole focus of the grandly view from the outside. It was truly special, and it's still special to have the privilege to be an American citizen with the opportunity to be of service to this world every single day. So, thank you United States of America. Land of the free indeed. 3!

Contents

Introduction

Welcome to my world of Philosophy! In this book, you will find very valuable information, including controversial topics that warrant discussion. I will deliver clever lines, movie/TV show references, song references, catchphrases, purposeful repetitions, metaphors, similes, personification, foreshadows, a few brain teasers, storytelling, and maybe enlighten you with some humor. I used every figurative language there is inside this book. Imagine a one-on-one personal conversation, a sermon, a lecture, a motivational speech, a standup special, and a poem combined together. The goal is to give you a complete experience, bringing this book to life.

Before you read, I want you to not think about anything negative in your life. Don't feel any type of way about anything you read or hear. Put all the emotions to the side. Listen to the words I'm saying whether you are listening to me on audiobook, listening to someone else read to you, or reading to yourself. Have an open mind while reading this book. This book will expand your mind and educate you about everything in life, including yourself and others, so you can improve internally and externally. "It's Right There" is to help you eliminate the world influences to become an "Unstoppable Force." A re-programming to never be programmed again! It's a whole life book in one. It will be so much easier for you to take accountability, accept responsibility, and serve a higher purpose by taking control of your life. You'll be able to find out your purpose, have self-awareness, and have ambition after this book. Success, happiness, and anything else that you deserve shall come your way after. I don't know exactly everything, but I strive to know more. I'm learning every day just like you can. Learning is unlimited, so learn. Start learning now!

Chapter 1

Signs

The signs are there every day for people to follow or listen to, whether in a metaphor or simile, etc. But the crazy thing is that sometimes the signs are right there in physical form for you to see. "It's Right There!"

Believe it or not, many are aware of possible signs, whether soulful or harmful. But it's in humans' nature to ignore them and continue what they set on doing. People can be their worst enemy and make life very difficult for themselves just by not following the signs, which can be called "self-sabotage." Sometimes, logical thinking can match the signs precisely. What are signs exactly, and what do they mean? I could go all day explaining in full detail about signs, but if you have common sense, there's no need. Signs are messages that inform you about a potential danger, whether fresh or like past experiences, or in some cases, a reassurance of greatness to come your way.

In most novels, signs are symbolic languages to foreshadow the future. Imagine knowing what could happen and fell short just because you ignored the signs. The Multiverse, Spirits, Creatures, and even sometimes your own soul can guide you to success and happiness, maybe even both. To get what you deserve or truly seek, you must be able to listen and follow. You must put your emotions and ego aside to achieve such greatness. Do not make it difficult for yourself. Like every wise man once said, "Work smarter, not harder." Having discipline and patience are required for it. To lead, you must follow first. You must learn from a master as a student to become the master. The greatest leaders in the world were the best listeners. Would you follow a king who never listens to his right-hand advice nor respects the advice from a member of his council, or would you follow a king who respects the advice from members of his council? Everyone should want to follow a king who can lead and listen when needed.

Therefore, observe everything and even take notes inside your head everyday like a mental note. Study people and their habits and pay attention to your surroundings until you have more knowledge. Don't rush the process; trust the process! Observation is the most important element in becoming the best at anything. Observation itself requires eye contact, open ears, and sometimes keeping a close distance. Sometimes, you have no idea how devastating or great your choice is until later. Sometimes, it comes very unexpectedly and can knock you off your boots. That's life for you, and you must learn from your mistakes. And time is everything! None of this exists without time. Time is the barrier, the gate, the impenetrable glue that keeps everything together or in line. Some events that are supposed to happen will happen eventually over time; it's inevitable. Time works whenever it wants and the way it wants. It serves no one, and everyone should think of time as the big boss.

Imagine playing video games in the early 2000s where you get frustrated losing over and over to the big boss. Eventually, in video games, you can beat the big boss. But unfortunately, you won't be able to defeat it in real life. Infinity to zero is the battle record against anything created from Matter unless you're Doctor Strange, who can keep looping over and over with the time stone in his possession. But you're not Doctor Strange, neither do you have the time stone. So, you never have as much time as you think. It's never in your favor. That's why you must pay attention to the signs and think about every decision before making it. I usually go by 3 methods when it comes to it. That's looking at the signs, thinking logically, and paying attention to the actions in the present. Almost everyone has all their senses, so if you have all five senses, there is no excuse not to sense anything. You can smell it, you can taste it, you can touch it, you can hear it, and you can definitely see it because "It's Right There!"

Chapter 2

Fear

Fear is an anti-life signal or spell that is implanted inside humans. It is something that can block you from seeing signs clearly; a mind, soul, and heart manipulator. How many really know about fear? When people mention fear, they think about phobias like being afraid of heights, spiders, going into deep water, etc. We can mention all of that, but fear is so much bigger, more influential, and more devastating than that. Fear is the biggest weapon used on humans. The deadliest weapon humans use against each other. The underline of almost every action committed by humans. Some may say they are not scared of anything, "try me," etc. Excuse my language, but that's some bullshit, honestly, because most people take action when afraid of something or when affected by similar past experiences. Negative effects from past experiences are called "trauma," and it haunts them like a nightmare. That's fear, "It's Right There!"

Fear can be considered the cause of all discrimination: Racism, Sexism, Religious Prejudice, you name it. Most discriminations are fear-based, not based on pure hate. A lot of folks get it mixed up, ultimately confusing themselves. Racism is the perfect example of fear-based discrimination. It's in human nature to react unpleasantly out of fear to a kind that looks different or acts differently than them. Everyone seems to overuse the word hate today when other factors are in place, such as rejection and fear. Black people, for example, feel like the White people who oppressed them loathe them when, really, they feared them.

You could argue that the oppression of Black people was strategic and did not solely rely on fear. Logically, slavery that existed in America could be an example of that, especially when considering what the economy was based on for a few centuries when the European settlers first landed in America. Whoever is a threat to you or your people, you will want to be their boss, keep them under, and put them in their place if you find them useful. That's what any conqueror or any survivor would do. It's survival of the fittest on Earth.

There are winners and losers, which is why the saying "life isn't fair" exists. I'm just saying, "It's Right There!"

It's basically the top dog in prison scenario, and it's more than fear. It's been a rivalry between the two since Ancient times. Slavery existed during Ancient times, and Egypt was a huge place for the slave trade at the time. You'll be very surprised to know who was in control of that. I mean, "It's Right There!" Sorry for the reality check, but different cultures have always been in competition. I'm a realist, and if you use common sense, you would know that any culture in a position of power would ensure their group of people have it better than everyone else. That's loyalty and putting your people first. That's why I don't believe in the term "White privilege" because anyone at the top would have it better than everyone else. So, in reverse, it could have been Black privilege, Hispanic privilege, Asian privilege, etc. I'm pretty sure other cultures would have done the same, too. They would deny it and say they would treat others better, but those are just words because, ultimately, everyone loves power once they have it.

If tested, so many will do whatever it takes to keep that power and never return to where they used to be. If the two cultures switched spots, there wouldn't be much of a difference. History has proven that mankind is power-hungry, and their true nature is revealed once in control without any authority over them. But I will say some are taught to hate another race without knowing the real reason for it, which is fear. The news and other media outlets help with the division. They always show race-baiting material, including being picky about the content they drop. It's always strategic. When it comes to race, they're not as positive, almost as if they don't want everyone to come together and be aware of their tactics. They fear that people will figure it out and come together to stop the divide completely. Speaking of their tactics, sometimes the media spreads rumors or exaggerates a particular subject to get people to hate someone they want. The agenda is so obvious, and most don't see the agenda because they believe the information just because it's the news; so, it must be fair and accurate they're thinking based on that.

You'll be surprised at how propaganda works. One thing the media loves presenting is fear. Fear is a huge propaganda tactic, the most prominent form of propaganda. The news and other media outlets raise the fear impulse higher than anyone. They know exactly how to create fear among the people, whether it comes to war, the usual politics, or a medical crisis like COVID-19. The pandemic would have never happened the way it did if it wasn't for the media involvement.

Their role was very important, but people must take full accountability on their own behalf. Regardless of anything the media told you or showed you, it's up to you to figure it out and decide what to do with the information. They're not responsible for how you react when only you control your words and actions. You are solely responsible for how you react. Despite everything I've said, I'm not against the news or other media outlets; let's be very clear. The news and other media outlets serve their purpose, and everyone is only doing their job. I have the utmost respect for everyone in that career field, as you should, too. Now, back to our daily programming.

When people fear impulses rise high, they make many illogical decisions. Some are even selfish, like toilet paper hoarders who leave no more for other people to buy. During the pandemic, people were even scared to walk outside and breathe in air properly. Some people even wore a mask inside their cars by themselves. Those individuals obviously fear very much; I doubt you can spread COVID-19 to yourself. But I won't judge. Fear can get the best of you. It's there, "It's Right There!"

The most underrated danger is an active shooter or armed robber full of fear. The more uncomfortable they are and the more they fear what can happen to them, the more dangerous they are. The last thing you want to do is increase the impulse of someone with a deadly weapon because it puts more people at risk of being severely wounded or killed. That's why, when negotiating, the cops ask questions on what the armed man would want on his list of demands. They do that to buy time and make the armed person feel comfortable so that they can apprehend or take them down unexpectedly without innocents getting hurt. It's a very strategic protocol to take control of the situation, and you must be very calculated and precise with only logical thinking that aligns with the protocol.

Speaking back on discrimination again, the most known form of discrimination in the entire world was "Anti-Semitism." Anti-Semitism was a term widely used during the rise of the Nazis during World War II. The Nazis feared the Jews very much. The Invasion of Poland was a significant historical event that unleashed the war Monster. They mass murdered innocent Jews in concentration camps and other invasions during this time, which is called "The Holocaust." The Jews had done nothing wrong to Hitler and his men, but Hitler's fear towards them sparked a fear among many other Germans around this time. Hitler feared what could happen in the future, and it's been considered that he had a personal hate against the Jews. It was a personal vendetta indeed, which usually stems from trauma. The holocaust was considered the biggest form of discrimination in humankind's History due to the body count and negative impact that it caused overall in such a short time frame.

The most underrated form of discrimination even applies to a Religion like Christianity, which is the biggest Religion in the world. Followers of that Religion discriminated against and killed more people than anyone in the world. Reading that may be hard to swallow, but it's the truth. If you don't believe it, look it up. "It's Right There!" The Catholic Persecutions, Ku Klux Klan, and many more throughout History. Let's be honest without singling out any Religion. There have been Religious wars with Christians against the Muslims, Muslims against the Jews, Christians against the Jews, and Catholic Christians having issues with the Pagans. But I'm not here to bash these Religions. Since I was a kid, my favorite speaker was a Religious one, Pastor Joel Esteen. I have the ultimate respect for committed Religious people more than anyone, especially certain Religious leaders with whom I have made connections. They are doing outstanding work in this world at the end of the day. I just wanted to use many examples of the power of fear because it's so destructive, like a cancer developing new forms of cancer.

Equality

I've mentioned the terms discrimination and privilege, but I want to touch up more on the term equality, connecting it to everything I've explained so far in this Chapter. Equality itself can be manipulated because many have hidden agendas behind it but speak so loudly and consistently about equality. A big reason why the American people wouldn't accept a communist or socialist government is because that means everyone would have the bare minimum, and people like having privilege or a chance to have it better than others.

Overall, everyone wants privilege no matter what race, sex, and sexual orientation they are.

America is so materialistic. People want to have the new Jordans, Gucci, Prada, a nice Mustang, a Lamborghini, a mansion, be in the VIP section, etc. They don't want to wear the cheapest low-quality shoes or drive a basic car. People in America love the luxury. For example, women strive to be equal, but they want to be better than men and have more control than men. That is a reason why they try to take control so much these days, no matter what. Same with trans-women, they don't necessarily want to be treated exactly like natural-born women. They want to be treated better. They want to be more valuable than natural-born women, the forever attraction in society's eyes. Trans women don't want to be just a trend or just a one-night stand; they want to be the highest quality of women on Earth to be someone's girlfriend or wife. Same as the LGBTQ+ movement in general, for years, people in that group have been bullied, harmed, and treated like less. Heterosexuality has been considered the normal standard for centuries, but we all know standards can change. So, the goal is for their standards to become the new normal.

After so much that they have overcome, why would they just want to be equal? They can eventually just take over when possessing strength in numbers and having powerful connections with resources. I'm just saying, "It's Right There!"

If people were ruled, at a certain point, they would come together, takeover, and rule themselves. Like Tom Segura said in his Netflix special "Mostly Stories" regarding another group, "why don't your group get their shit together, and then you can ascend to the top, and then you can oppress other people." That's a fair point. But "human's nature is to get in there and fight, straighten them out, show them what they're made of," just like Pastor Joel said. Whether you believe it or not, it doesn't matter; "It's Right There!"

Why Make Yourself an Enemy?

Humans are the biggest threat to themselves, and the percentage of that is increasing rapidly. They will destroy themselves if they aren't led the right way and/or if they're disobedient. They can't have too much freedom because they don't do all the right things with more freedom. For example, most women today would rather keep messing with men who aren't beneficial for them rather than dating men who are crucially beneficial. To know that women finally get more freedom and get to choose their men, unlike women for centuries before, and still, they actively choose low-quality men who harm them physically, mentally, or emotionally. 3! That's the perfect example because people don't know what's best for them even if "It's Right There!" Some know but would still reject it. Perhaps the trauma caused by one of their past relationships affected them hard, and they never truly recovered from it. You can be the perfect guy, and they would not believe it, so they will get rid of you before you further prove yourself. They have been hurt or disappointed too many times to the point where they've stopped believing, as if it's impossible to have such a grand life. Damn! It could have been grand, but with a slam. Grand slam!

Many would say they want someone rare or different per se, but that person who's so different psychologically scares them. This fear may stem from the perceived unreadability of such individuals, leading to concerns about potential harm. Some individuals may also realize their own psychological issues and fear causing harm to others. Studies have proven men fear the most in general, especially when it comes to love, and that is why they do the most hurtful shit in the entire world. A woman can get hurt once and try again multiple times with love. A guy gets hurt once and most likely gives up immediately, becoming the worst in the dating pool. That's pathetic and weak if you ask me.

I'm just saying, "It's Right There!" Women are stronger and more fearless than the world gives them credit for. Those who have been hurt don't know what to do with the person they've been wishing for or deserve. They start to question themselves like they don't deserve it, or in some cases, it's like they rebooted and don't even know themselves anymore. This phenomenon can be linked back to the concept of self-sabotage, as individuals with too much freedom may grapple with inner turmoil.

One surprisingly significant thing I've found is that people don't know the real consequences of their actions. It's like they're not afraid of them because they've been receiving light consequences. Usually, some get warnings, a light sentence, a tolerable beating, a fine, or just a slap on the wrist. People have more privilege than they think, especially Americans. I personally saw many people steal items from Walmart, and people joked about doing that on social media. There wouldn't be many jokes if people were taught proper lessons. That's an example of how light consequences are today. Consequences are not taken seriously at all! Nobody will learn to stop doing foul activity if they aren't receiving actual consequences. People feel like they could do whatever they want and get away with it, or that their unjustified actions won't significantly negatively affect them. It's like people don't respect Karma or the law because they have been babied. I'm just saying, "It's Right There!"

In History, for centuries in many places throughout the world, people received real consequences; some were very harsh. People got their hands cut off for stealing, heads cut off for treacherous acts, some got hanged for breaking the law, and some got shot in the head for other crimes too. I'm not saying America and every other country should return to that, but there must be more real consequences where people can learn never to violate again. Some foreign countries still have ways to give real consequences in this day and age, though. Limitations are definitely needed when establishing order because limitations balance out humans and keep them in line. Respect, honor, and honesty among humans used to be so much higher back then. Now, all 3 of these qualities just hit an all-time low because of the lack of limitations and real consequences in this new generation.

A lot of people today are so selfish and impatient. Some people do what they do because they can't handle freedom and can't handle responsibilities, so they self-sabotage as a defensive mechanism. Humans may even push away/ reject new people to protect themselves when, in some cases, it's the opposite because some of those new folks can be exactly what they needed the whole time. "If you are full of light, then you are aggravating their demons," as a Christian would say. People are so affected by the past, which is a huge sign of fear, that they won't believe anything or anyone that can complete them. They have been so destroyed that almost everything seems false to them, and they get instant flashbacks from that trauma, with plenty of people getting hurt by that. It's like a tornado picking up in speed and strength while taking whatever may come its way, leaving catastrophic damage to the things it picked up, including the paths it crossed. People are so damaged that they damage themselves significantly, like they're punishing themselves, which can be called "self-hate." Believe it or not, some may even fear themselves so much to become the main antagonist in their own story. For example, lovers or friends lie instead of telling people the truth when, in fact, lying makes it worse and is considered a negative look on the person, creating distrust between both parties. A lie can soothe their feelings, but it won't soothe them when they require proper healing. The truth may hurt their feelings, but it won't hurt them entirely. Lies hurt your future self, while truths protect your future self. Tell the truth! That's the key, grab the key, "It's Right There!"

Even when it comes to bonds, there are many who would rather push away someone so genuine to deal with someone who's fake and a future threat to them. The tradeoff from that can be considered a form of self-hate. They could act like they don't care and let that genuine person walk away to hold on to their pride. That's very absurd! Never let your pride get in the way of your blessing. Facing the expected hurt is what they would rather face than the unexpected hurt. That expected hurt gives them more of a comfort psychologically. The fear of the unexpected is a killer and is considered the number one fear dealing with connections. People's choices on who they pick as a lover or friend extremely help define who they are. Big moments are when people reveal their true nature or what they are masking. You'll be surprised by the type of masks the ones closest to you wear. They could be masked for years, and you wouldn't even notice.

This is a loveless generation who claim they are full of love but don't properly love themselves. Fear is controlling humans' souls. It's like a dark cloud that consumes or absorbs any person in its path. Once fully consumed by fear, they spiral out of control and may never be the same again. They will throw negative energy at someone they truly love or care about, which is a textbook lack of emotional intelligence. In some cases, a particular individual will shit on someone else when they are really talking about themselves. My mother, for example, feared me having a better life and having no communication with her in the future to the point where she kind of manifested it by saying, "you are this, you're going to do that," etc. and followed up with mistreating me like I'm not much in her eyes. That's an eye-opener for those who need to visualize to understand it all better.

The fact many young men and women would rather hurt anyone they encounter just to avoid being hurt again exemplifies how fear is deeply rooted in this society today. They were tortured to the point they became the torturer. Where do they draw the line? What's so crazy is people brag about being toxic or so destructive and sometimes laugh about it. I've always wondered what's so funny about not being healed, being difficult, and creating drama instead of bringing peace. What the world has turned into? The most ironic part is people love hearing more songs about hate than love. Instead of breaking the cycle, they would rather keep it going and make it worse for others. The more people fear, the more destructive people become, and the more their character takes a hit in morality while also descending as a soul.

Fear in personal attachments to another person is often expressed in that "used to be" line. It's the most common line people consistently use regarding someone changing negatively. They'll say, "well, he was amazing," "she was so full of life," etc. These people are stuck in the past and have a fear of losing or having to get rid of the person who consistently talks to them. They fear being alone and fear that the person they were so intimate with isn't their special person anymore. Seeing that 180-degree change or switch up of that individual brings up the fear that they will never find the one, soulmate, etc. Denial is a hypnotizing force implanted in their brain, heart, and soul, causing them to function in a way that's far from reality. Denial is not accepting the obvious truth because someone is too scared to accept it. People start to question, "is this really happening?" but it's up to them to realize that it's happening. It's tough for them because that means their fear just became a reality. To paint a picture, denial is turning your head away from that fear that's right in front of your face trying to make eye contact with you, or you are pretending like that fear isn't there at all, like John Cena. If you didn't get that reference, you know nothing, like Jon Snow. If you didn't get that Jon Snow reference also, then I have no faith in you. Now, let's talk about being emotionally driven.

Emotionally Driven

Logical thinking goes hand-in-hand with fairness. Emotional thinking goes hand-in-hand with unfairness/bias. I know these lines will go over some people's heads. Those same people will even shake their heads in disagreement. People need to understand that most logical decisions are going to hurt people's feelings, but its fair, especially in the long run. Let's say you work at a job. You're always working hard and always respectful, but someone else doesn't work as hard as you, nor take their work seriously. The other person can get away with some things and get more praise than you. That's an example of bias, which is unfair to you. The connection between your coworker and the boss/bosses gives them an advantage. Most likely, it's a personal thing and has nothing to do with the job. They like that coworker, but not you, due to their feelings. So, if there are decisions that are made logically, which is overall fair to everyone in the long run, then you shouldn't be upset. If you get very upset and never accept it, then you're showing how selfish you are. Your emotional drive is going to increase, making you say hateful things and do so much damage. You fear not having or losing the power, so you're doing and saying everything for you to have the power/ have it your way. Don't feel too ashamed to become The Burger King; it's expected of you. It's in your nature. You're human! Emotional drive, privilege, fear! You see, I told you, "It's Right There."

One important thing I will say, proven to be true in most cases, is that being emotionally driven is dangerous. Being emotionally driven can cause a lot of destruction, especially if you already have plenty of problems. Adding new issues with the original ones in place makes it more catastrophic for yourself internally, and for the ones around you. It can reflect on the outside of you, which is your appearance, if anyone has that deep sense of reading an individual. Sometimes, it's easy to tell because "It's Right There!" A very familiar part of emotional drive is the term I call "fuck it" decisions. These "fuck it "decisions are the type of decisions people make when they are very eager or apathetic to do something in that moment. Usually, they think about it for one second and then follow through. They actually say "fuck it" with their mouth or say it in their head as they commit these actions. The "fuck it" comes from the fact that they're not caring about anything else no matter what, a very careless decision. These decisions are always among the worst decisions these folks make because logic and consequences that will affect them or others go out the window. Some guys make "fuck it" decisions when it comes to sending an explicit photo or having sex without a condom when they're so quick to just have sex with someone. And that's how some catch cases, catch people's fists to their faces, catch diseases, or make babies. A lot of babies today were made by "fuck it" decisions, the main reason why there are so many broken households. Do not make "fuck it" decisions.

Emotional decisions like "fuck it" decisions are the cause of regret. Regret usually comes after making illogical choices in emotionally driven moments that hurt your future self or someone else. When people make logical decisions, they usually have no regrets because it was the best decision made. If the results weren't what they wanted after a logical decision, they can accept it and live with it forever. You won't always be right, but you'll be satisfied knowing you had a clear judgment and have control of your emotions. Use your brain and have a care. Overall, emotionally driven people are the most impatient, undisciplined, and illogical people in the world. Most super villains are emotionally driven, like Anakin Skywalker, also known as "Darth Vader." If you are not familiar with "Star Wars," Anakin had the potential to be a great Jedi, but his fear and his emotional drive led him to the dark side to become Darth Vader. He ended up killing many innocents with his light saber and even destroyed planets. Usually, the super villain's goal to destroy the world or galaxy usually stems from how people treated them. It goes back to how much pain people caused them, which explains the tortured become the torturer scenario I've recently stated. So, if you're not in control of your emotions, then you're a liability to everyone and a danger to maybe the whole world if you get powerful enough with the emotional drive installed in your motives. Kill the emotional drive if you don't want to be a complete Monster. The emotional drive, I see it! Go kill it, "It's Right There!"

Being Free

Before I close this Chapter, I briefly want to discuss what being free is. Many people get so confused and never learn what it really means. Most people also think they're free when, in fact, they're not. It's a test, a simulation, a game. Humans are basically like test subjects until they break out of the lab. Being free is knowing yourself, realizing who you truly are, knowing your purpose, and seeing the world from the outside. People don't really know what being free is. They think not being told what to do or being able to fuck anyone, go anywhere, or do whatever they like is freedom; when it's not. Don't get offended by any of this. Let that motivate you to stand out and become powerful. Turn on God/Goddess mode and be confident in it.

True freedom is found in fulfilling one's purpose without fear, eliminating the shackles that hold individuals back. This process empowers individuals to stay true to their code, unburdened by the weight of fear. Doing what you need to do without even a self-interest is being free. As fear is conquered, the soul becomes radiant and powerful. Living without worry, free from the haunting echoes of the past or anxiety about future harm, signifies triumph over fear. Defeating fear will make you a better human being, and it will prepare you for your ascension to become something much bigger. Break those chains and get yourself out of the loop. Being free is basically not being a slave to the world's influence completely. You literally are now out of this world, "It's Right There!"

Chapter 3

Communication

Silence! Listen to the words that are coming out of someone's mouth. Be respectful and always make eye contact. If a person is talking nonsense, simply "AIR" it out: acknowledge, ignore, and resume. Everyone still deserves to be heard at the end of the day. Criminals who are about to serve a long sentence or receive the death penalty even get a chance to speak; it's a human right. The lack of listening is so high among civilization; "a bunch of hardheads," as the older generation would say. Just as I mentioned in the first Chapter, listening is key. If you can't do that, then you shouldn't lead. Let's talk about verbal messages, which include lessons you can apply in life. Those same verbal messages where people can learn and add more knowledge to their brains sometimes cause them to pay more attention to who's saying it instead of the actual message. It doesn't matter what Religion you believe in or how annoying someone can be by teaching you something that you don't want to hear; you should still listen to the message. You may have heard it, but you didn't listen to it. There's a difference between hearing and listening. Listening is paying attention to every word. Hearing is just focusing on the rhythm or vibrations of someone's voice when it comes to conversation. So, once again, listen to the message. That message is key, and keys unlock things. That message will significantly help you on your journey in this human experience.

The "WORD" is the "WORD" regardless. When you are having that same conversation, imagine a voice without a person in physical form. Speak if you have a voice; be heard, and make sure they listen to you. In today's world, people barely speak and have many improper ways to communicate; texting is one of them. The most used form of communication today is texting. I'll be frank about texting; no sugarcoating. If we are talking about getting to the point, well, texting is drawing circles and wasting people's time. It's so ironic how a society that doesn't like reading with a short attention span prefers communicating through text, which requires reading and waiting repeatedly in a cycle. Realistically, most texters can't read; they skim. These skimmers wouldn't read everything you've sent them, including missing out on important key words to understand the message truly. People truly get exposed on their reading comprehension skills when you text them. The contradiction is so high. You might as well speak or forever hold your peace. You could talk about everything in one minute on the phone or in person compared to texting someone for an hour straight. Real people will call you up or see you or make time to socialize in person if they're not far away distance-wise. Fake ones, unconfident ones, and even ones who can't properly communicate will always try to text you.

If someone has all five senses and can't properly communicate with you, then they still have problems to figure out. People tend to hide behind a keyboard instead of speaking their minds, giving their real energy and tone. People are too accustomed to the keyboard. Texting is the easiest and most convenient way to communicate, but it's the least effective. If you really want to get to know someone, you must speak to them and/ or be around them. You can't detect someone's tone through a text 100%, identify someone's intentions through a text, or sense someone's energy through a text. Most importantly, you can't build trust through text because the most important aspect of trust is eye contact. Eye contact is everything when speaking to someone. Body language, appearance, and eye contact inform so much about a person. It's terrifying to want to build up with someone who doesn't really speak to you the authentic way. They put themselves in danger by not being around someone or speaking to them by voice. When texting, you have so much time to think of whatever. You may just tell people whatever they want to hear instead of the truth. In real-time, it's different; people get exposed in real-time. If you're a consistent observer, you could read lies with your eyes like it's nothing. You could pick up on people's patterns and certain behaviors in person, but you can't pick up any of that through typing. You could be dealing with a psycho; you never know. The fact that people fear so much but would build a connection through text is mind-blowing and makes no sense.

Going back to time being everything also applies to texting because you could text someone for months, and then when you finally meet them or speak, they seem like a whole different person. Some start to see how unattractive that person is once they finally make it more real communication-wise. Therefore, there was time wasted just because they didn't do things the most effectively. They settled instead of setting the tone of making things happen in real life so as not to waste any time. People are too comfortable texting, and I learned that no matter what, people stick to what they are used to. I've met people who lived around the corner from me and wanted to text back and forth instead of having a face-to-face, in-person conversation. That's how low communication has gotten today in quality. Fear still plays a factor in texting once again because we have people who will ghost someone instead of giving someone closure and properly ending things. That ghosting behavior is not honorable at all. People ghost others because they are too scared to tell someone the truth to properly end things, knowing they would like someone to inform them instead of doing that to them. People fear being the villain, so they run away from giving a proper send-off. Social media is similar; people just block someone so quickly like they never mattered in the first place.

People can never grow if they don't practice having class, and people can't grow if another person doesn't know what they need to work on. That's why it's best to face problems head-on and fully communicate to have an understanding, which is a proper ending like many had in person for centuries before social media and texting. One huge problem today is that people bring up important information at the very last minute, which are significant things they should have brought up from the start. Having a boyfriend or girlfriend and making people aware if they're not attracted to the opposite sex are perfect examples of withheld important information. Many send mixed signals today, especially teens and young adults. Whatever that's important, you must reveal it regardless of how you feel. If you feel like it isn't important to you, then you should still discuss it because it can be important to that other person. The other party deserves to be aware, and it's fair. The hidden info that should have been brought up from the start could have wasted that person's time if they were truly considering building a special connection with you. Another problem with communication today is the lack of effort. People want to talk to someone when it's convenient for them, no matter how much it's affecting the other person who's actively communicating, giving so much effort. Communication is supposed to be a two-way street, 50/50. Some don't realize that the other person's time is important too, and you can't play with other people's time. You can't always have it your way; it's not Burger King. You're dealing with real people, and people have feelings, including other important things in their lives. You have to be fair, so don't treat someone who's showing so much dedication like they are beneath you. I've learned from my studies of the many encounters that I've had with women that a woman will make time for you if she really likes you with no excuses. So why would certain individuals waste people's time by playing someone like a game? They do it because it makes them feel powerful in a way, and they are just following what someone did to them. Mirroring the one or ones who mistreated them. Why would you do something that you wouldn't like done to you? People could never answer that.

The most shocking thing is that men and women would rather want attention from someone who doesn't even care about them but would neglect and play the very individuals who genuinely care about them from a communication standpoint. Why would you not go hard and give all the effort to the ones who are giving the actions of a true lover or friend? It all goes back to what happened in people's past and the type of environments that they surrounded themselves in. Speaking of that, I discovered that about 53% of the minds today hang with people who don't want them to be better or grow. They want them to be stuck in the same place as them or be beneath them. Around 74% of teens and young adults ages 18 to 22 consistently trust and mix their energy with negative influences that are ultimately not their friends but their enemies. Enemies want to keep you closer to keep an eye on you, hoping you don't surpass them and will keep you away from your best self. Opponents know how to act accordingly and are underrated for making an ally seem like the opposite. These dark, negative individuals know how to capture and control these lost souls who are broken people. They love doing what they do.

Ones who will always make time for you or ride for you should be fully embraced while you get rid of the false believers. Ones who have nothing to hide are completely open and honest, thinking of the long term. Short term and live-in-the-moment to have fun types of people are the ones who want to use you as much as they can or need to feed on you. If an individual has no expectations of someone, then they're obviously telling you that they are completely broken and don't want to be disappointed anymore. Anyone speaking to them can identify that, and that's when you know they stopped caring about almost everything, including their future/ well-being in general. You should know that's a sign you received about their fear just by their communication.

Communication today has created so many problems like bipolar disorder, social anxiety, etc. Some have bipolar disorder due to their environments, and the dialogue spoken throughout those environments has affected them. It can be so hard dealing with a friend or lover who's bipolar, I can relate to it myself. Imagine being with someone who spirals emotionally and tries to break up with you every day, then forgets about it. You should get what I'm saying, it was difficult indeed. It's a battle, especially when someone never got diagnosed with it or doesn't even realize they may have it and/or just doesn't want to get the proper help.

Also, many people today have social anxiety due to being glued to Technology like texting or just playing games all day and not actively interacting with people. It's very important in life to speak. You'll never be heard, understood, or respected without a voice. Weak people hate strong minds. If you have a voice, speak what you believe in with strong conviction. Tell people how you feel, what you think, or inform them of your wisdom right then and there on the spot. Some things must be said right there. That is why it came out of nowhere, and you felt that pressure on your chest because it's meant to come out in that moment. Time is letting you know it's time to release. Come on now; "It's Right There!" Release! Actively talking is a part of the everyday life in the career world. It's normal and has been normal for centuries, until now for some, obviously. If you have limitations speaking due to serious conditions like being unable to speak, then I understand, but if you can, then there's no excuse. Be confident, kill that fear, and be around people. Speak! Your voice, "It's Right There!"

Chapter 4

Lust and Love

Lust is one of the most powerful weapons to influence the world. The promotion of sex is everywhere, online and in person. Lust is taking over many minds today, especially teens and young adults. It's the second leading underline to humans' actions in this world, and its power is only increasing. Lust is getting more love than actual natural love, which is a gigantic problem that will only be more difficult to stop. You have porn everywhere, whether on porn sites, magazines, porn movies, sex scenes in normal genres of shows or movies, sexual content being shown on social media apps/ websites, and videos or pictures of sexual teasing between people. As a man who watched porn in the past, I can say porn is sabotaging society. It's not essential for people's minds even though people enjoy it and learn sexual positions from it. Porn overall manipulates people in many ways, and people can explain themselves if you ask them. They know how powerful it is because, ultimately, it's the biggest influencer when it comes to lust. Think about it like this, Pornhub is in the top 5 in one of the most viewed websites there are as of today, along with XVideos making the top 10.

Even though the porn industry leads the way in lust promotion, the porn industry, including websites like Pornhub and XVideos, is not responsible for whatever you decide to think about or act on. You are solely responsible for whatever you decide to think about and act on. Whatever you do with your body, whether on self or with others, is up to you. You are in control of every aspect of you. Do not blame pornographic websites, any apps, pornographic magazines, sexual content on TV, or the government in general. You must take accountability for your part. Now, back to our daily programming.

Believe it or not, there are more people in lust than in love. Even I fell victim to lust because it consumed my mind for years, and I've honestly hated lusting; that's how powerful lust is. Lust can make you do crazy things, and it can block you from seeing people's true harmful nature. It can block you from seeing how unattractive a person can be overall. The scary truth is that America is the biggest influencer when it comes to lust. America has the most influence in the entire world when it comes to anything in general. Sex, sex, sex; all over the radio, on people's minds, and blasting inside their speakers.

The Sex Agenda on Women

Number 1: People are not sex objects! But many influencers are working so hard to make that a reality. For example, the feminist movement originally was meant for women to be respected, treated as an equal, to work in the same workplace as men, and for men to get to know them for them, and they were really against being sexualized in any type of matter. The original feminists were so against the idea of being a sex symbol. They only wanted to be treated like a lady. That original stance has died, and the new feminists completely undid everything / went against everything the original feminists stood for. They let the social media influencers, the media, models, and other women who were already a sex symbol campaign for the new feminist movement. They basically let the sellouts takeover and brainwash the new wave of women. It can be argued those same women sold out to kill the original movement stance for money and fame. Sex sells so much today, and it was always men in America who planned to sexualize women completely. If you don't believe me, you can research all of that also. Think about it real hard. Women are being less respected because of the shift. Some women leave the workplace or never enter the workplace just to do OnlyFans or sell sexual content in other ways. A large portion of women would rather have men pay them to see their bodies instead of having a normal conversation to get to know them, and a lot of women now promote sexual work or embody being a sex freak more than ever in History. That's everything that original feminists didn't want to happen.

Women for centuries were forced into sex work, and 95% of them would have never done it willingly if they had more freedom or had options such as having the same job opportunities as men. Today, society has brainwashed the new generation of women to want to be a sex symbol automatically and willingly, programming to feed the agenda of lust. Men wanted women to shut up and show their titties and ass; now that's a reality. There's no freedom in doing exactly what they wanted you to do in the first place, whether on your own accord or not. You may make a lot of money, but you're a slave to the world influence of lust. "It's Right There!" As far as body positivity is concerned, it's really for horny men to get off with their high impulse of lust. Who do you think is running all these social media pages and monitoring all these feeds? Who do you think is always quick to comment under and like the body positivity posts? Men! See, I told you, "It's Right There!" It was all a trap from the very start, but a lot of women look up to these beautiful women with money and fame, wanting to be them so much.

Although that's true, famous women are not responsible for how you feel or what you decide to do with your body. You are solely responsible for how you feel or decide to do with your body. They are just playing their role just like any other influencer of the many world influences. You must take accountability as it is your life because you control your life, not them. Now, back to our daily programming.

One big fact in this day and age of social media is that everyone follows the trend and doesn't want to be left out under any circumstances. Why is body positivity promoted more than women's fashion style or more than a woman's beauty in her face, hair, or smile? A smile is contagious and can make people's day by giving so much positive energy. It shows a big sign of confidence. A woman's eyes can be hypnotizing to a man, her wardrobe tells a man that she has style, the hair compliments the face and wardrobe. Overall, a beautiful face makes a man blush, especially if she has an attractive voice to add on. Even if we talk about body, you can show that off in a very nice outfit or dress. There's really no need to show a bunch of skin to showcase how great a woman's figure is. Honestly, around 80% of men would fuck anything and anyone regardless. That's shallow as far as morals and self-respect as a man is concerned, but there are lots of men like that.

I am personally disappointed by how lustful men can be. I once saw a Facebook post about a choice between having sex with Princess Fiona from the movie, "Shrek," whether in the day or night. Many guys said Princess Fiona at night just because she's thicker. If you're not familiar with the movie "Shrek," Princess Fiona had a curse where she turns into an Ogre at nighttime. Why would any man have sex with an Ogre? They live in swamps and bathe in mud, according to that fairytale. So, these men would fuck a dirty Creature just because she has some thickness to her. That should be very distasteful for women. When most men think about sex, all the logic goes out the window, and beauty doesn't even matter. You could be ugly in the face with a body, and men still would have sexual relations with you just because you have a body. So, in conclusion, showing you have a body is not that uplifting if you really think about it. So, women please higher the standards and choose men who lust less. Let your overall beauty of you flourish. Be a princess, a queen, then turn into a Goddess. Carry yourself like your existence is the attraction and the only thing that matters. If you highlight the body more than anything, that's all these men will think about when it comes to you with the high-quality men naturally assuming that's all you have to offer.

The Scary Truth

I realized people of today over-display a specific thing to attract others because they are insecure about other factors of themselves, like all forms of intelligence or personality. So, for a woman, it could be showing off your body and revealing a lot of skin in most of your social media posts. For men, it could be showing their muscles, cash, or even materialistic things like a chain or car. Men showing that, reveals their insecurities on feeling like they're only physically strong or possess loads of money. These men are insecure about their emotional or general intelligence and other factors that make a great man, like personality and the will to serve as a trusting lifelong partner. Most women focus on those muscle guys' muscles, being mostly attracted to their physical bodies in general with the idea that they may lack intelligence. In some cases, they already concluded that these men aren't the romantic type of guys. Plenty of women also think that men who are flashy with money or expensive things will be willing to spend so much on them and that these men have no confidence in other parts of them. You're not showcasing yourself when you show the flashy things. You're showcasing the items and not even yourself. You weren't a huge factor at all. So, there is never a surprise when these rich men lovers leave them after being broke or having way less than they originally had. It's because they didn't get with you for you. They were attracted to the money and the lifestyle they could have due to your money. That's your fault. I'm just saying, "It's Right There!"

There are a lot of unconfident, weak men too. I will get on everyone and not target a specific group. Nobody's safe! No one can get better unless they listen to the truth about what they need to work on, which means even knowing something negative about themselves to improve. I've mentioned that in

Chapter 3 for a reason. That negative can turn into a positive once they are aware of the negative and then make the proper adjustments to change it. Constructive criticism is also necessary for your evolution. Put your feelings aside and receive the truth that someone is conveying about you. That's the key, grab the key, "It's Right There!"

Women may think showing the body is a sign of confidence. That could be true internally, referring to someone's feelings, but men think those women aren't confident if they must showcase all of that to be confident. Men say, "She doesn't love herself," and some automatically label her as someone to have sex with or to lust on for ejaculation. Highlight that you're more than just a body. If you don't, then that's how men will treat you, like you're another body to add to their body count. The set up is there, "It's Right There." It's crazy how a sex icon would say, "A real man would," when they never had a real man who didn't lust over them and loved them as a person overall while respecting themselves as a man. A real man with principles is attracted to a woman who respects herself and carries herself as a lady to a certain degree with high standards. Yes, a woman's beauty can attract a real man, of course. But what's going to really make him pursue that woman to be his woman is her mind, heart, soul, and the will to do what needs to be done.

Why should a man respect a woman who doesn't respect herself? That's like trying to build a contradicting relationship. I noticed that many young adult women today would rather smoke or drink and chill than want a guy to properly know about them, which includes having real conversations and asking each other important questions. The same issue applies to young adult men too. They all feel like they're being interrogated, but you must know certain things to see how someone really is and not waste your time. There is so much that matters that can be very problematic later. That's like hiring anyone for a job because they seem cool and have the potential to be a hard worker, but you didn't even interview them. You must lack care or be desperate if the qualification for the role is too low, and you're just hiring anybody. Don't try the Amazon Warehouse hiring process when it comes to love. I'm just saying, "It's Right There!" No offense to Amazon because Jeff Bezos is a genius. I love shopping on Amazon, especially for books. You know exactly what I'm talking about regarding this reference. If you know, you know. You shouldn't just hire anybody and get intimately close with someone if they aren't a great candidate to receive the role of your lifelong partner. You see what I did there? I told you, "It's Right There!"

Another thing is, you shouldn't have to see people's reactions or get compliments from lustful men who don't care about you to make you feel beautiful. You should know that you're beautiful and look amazing already. You should only be seen by worthy people who see all of you. Most men prefer a woman who hasn't shown herself to everybody. Some won't admit it, but it makes it uncomfortable for many men to lust over their girlfriend/wife knowing all of these men have already seen everything underneath their wife/girlfriend's clothing, if they truly considered their woman to be special to them. I know some will disagree. You probably have a cuck, not a man; there's a difference. I'm just saying, "It's Right There."

A lot of relationships are lust-based. Believe it or not, many people are in relationships with a friend with benefits, not a husband or wife. You can have fun, which some call a "good time," but, likely, you will no longer have a "good time" with that person if you can't get through the hard times. People who can survive the hard times and not forget being the very best are lifelong partners. Many today can't handle the pressure; they can't handle real commitment at all. It's proven every single day among mankind when an individual gets bored with their lover or feels like they have options. It can be described as thinking there is someone better, so they look forward to finding another who interests them. They slowly build up with this person, and if their relationship gets harder or hits a rough patch; they already have the next person they plan to date or sleep with. Some are too accustomed to going from one person to another or simply want to move on to the next partner. Many women discreetly do this, and I can confirm this because I've been the guy friend they became interested in. A lot of men do the same; they just aren't smart about it. Women are very clever when it comes to this, while men make it so obvious. Some are ready to move on, even if their relationship is not even failing. In most cases, it's all connected to fear, where people strike first and try to take control.

Speaking of women again, the hard truth is that around 60% of women find a committed man more attractive than a single man. It makes no sense why, but somehow, it appears to be that way. I've witnessed, and even others have witnessed women flirting with another woman's man. Most have the intention

28

of taking another woman's man. Some, in fact, have been successful in taking another woman's man. But why would you want to be with someone who left their woman for you? If they can do that to a great woman they're in love with, what makes you think they won't do that to you? You're not unstoppable in this scenario because they will do the same thing to you with time. The time is near; there goes Karma. Oh shit! Damn! See, I told you, "It's Right There!"

Men are more into having sex with someone's woman without being in a relationship with them at all. They even brag about having sex with a man's woman to their friends or even mention it in a song, which a lot of rappers do. Why do you feel so proud to break up a bond and/or family to feed your ego? That's very absurd! Guys must be better at that because it affects men overall when it comes to love mentally and emotionally. Also, I really do believe some women think single men are not capable enough to be real lovers like it's the main reason why they're single. A woman could go for a committed man to get a man that's already proven to be boyfriend and husband material, or they could be going for that type of man just because that man is barely sweating them. People of today like to chase for some reason. One too many women chase after guys who are unavailable or not much interested in them/ don't care much. Also, some men chase women who will use them for their kindness or money or wouldn't give them their full time on any day. I would say there are a few men out of many that will try to take another man's woman also. That's another example of selfishness people have today. They're not looking at the bigger negative impact or Karma to come their way later in the future. We're all connected, even love-wise. It will circle back to you at some point. Wrong is wrong, but where do people draw the line?

Realistically, there are certain individuals that will tell you that they don't care to your face or lie straight to your face. If they do that, run away as far as possible. To lie to someone straight in their face repeatedly, is one of the most effective ways to disrespect someone and to be untrustworthy even to themselves. They want what they want. But sometimes what you want isn't logical, fair, nor soulful for you in the long run. Some wants may seem so amazing for you temporarily, but in the end it will mess you up and expire. What you want is to make you feel better, but not necessarily better for you. Your wants aren't always essential; most are the complete opposite. Lust is a perfect example of a want. It manipulates your soul into thinking it's soulful, gradually altering your mental state. Speaking on commitment again, this world today, compared to generations before, is the least dependable on commitment. Some would sacrifice their whole family or someone special to them for a one-night-stand or multiple-night-stands. They want to feel better from someone else, no matter what it costs them in these emotionally driven moments of high impulses of lust and pain. They do it all for nothing because that's usually what they end up with. Nothing! "It's Right There!"

In the aftermath, their reaction can extremely define who they are. If they own up to it willingly with regret, they may be decent. If they try to hide it the whole time without any regret or react distastefully when confronted, then that defines their incapability of being a quality partner for anyone. Many are terrified of commitment even after putting themselves in a committed situation. Why build a connection with someone if you're not willing to commit 100%? Lay it all on the line because you're involved in a union/bond with someone else. There are another person's feelings and thoughts besides yours; you must think about that. Having emotional intelligence is required for a successful relationship or partnership. In anything dealing with love, emotional intelligence must be a skill for you to have. And even though some may talk about commitment so much like that's what they need or want and are ready for, they get exposed when it meets them face to face in big moments.

Even when it comes to marriage, people look at all the glamour than the actual commitment itself. They pay attention to the fancy wedding dresses and all the other materialistic things you usually see at a wedding. People are so obsessed with that moment on that day that they're not truly ready for anything else. They even pay attention to the honeymoon between the husband and wife, which includes the vacation and all the unlimited sex that comes with it. The problem is that they forget about something very significant. The most significant thing they're not thinking about is the actual words within the vows. In movies, they reveal all the emotions leading up to the kiss. They show the eagerness of the groom or bride to skip the vows and seal the kiss. That shows you people's priorities when it comes to marriage. "It's Right There!"

Heal!

Now, I will discuss people who recently just got out of a relationship, engagement, or marriage. About 23% take time to themselves and properly heal before having any relations, including sexual relations with anyone. On the flip side, 77% of people today don't properly heal and do the exact opposite. Many will go from one relationship to the next repeatedly without much time in between. It's obvious those individuals didn't heal; they just keep going to the next, hoping maybe someone out there can heal them completely, instead of doing the work for themselves. But what's the point of building a connection with someone if you're not going to stick it out? Either stick with one person grinding it out or stay single to heal and get your life together, which requires no sexual intercourse with anyone, either. Stay in the house if you have to, without inviting company over. Give yourself a lot of time with that. Once you feel like you're ready, then try a relationship again. Just make sure when you try a relationship again, be super picky to make sure it's the right person you can last with.

Now, other ones who have just been hurt or extremely heartbroken would go on this new term called the "hot girl"/ "city boy" phase or, as they used to call it, the "hoe"/ "player" phase. Instead of breaking the cycle, they tend to do things that don't help them ultimately, internally or externally, which keeps the cycle on repeat. They let lust consume them completely and enjoy it no matter how many negative effects take place in the aftermath. They would rather use a distraction, also known as a "coping mechanism," than do what needs to be done. They lack discipline and patience heavily. Doing this can prevent you from healing 100%, dampen your healing power, and affect your next relationship or whatever connection you eventually will build with someone else. The short term may seem so different at the time, but you're damaging yourself in the long run. It's never worth it to harm your future self.

Sometimes, all people can think about is the short term in these emotional moments. "Fuck it" decisions and lust go hand-in-hand also. Many people catch sexual diseases from the high impulses of lust, besides creating babies, which I've already mentioned before. People are so quick to say, "fuck it," and have unprotected sex, meaning wearing no condoms, then catching sexual diseases in the aftermath. Sexually Transmitted Diseases like Gonorrhea, Genital Herpes, Chlamydia, and more damaging diseases like HIV can be spread to you. These diseases are considered uncurable and can ruin the rest of your sex life and love life in general. Stay protected, and don't have sex unless you plan on being with someone forever. Many people's first action on their agenda is to mess around and so-called "be free." They do this instead of

31

healing or working on problems or habits they still need to work on/ fix. You know exactly how to break the cycle. You know what your soul really wants you to do. The steps to your future happiness and being the best version of yourself are close by. You can't see it? How can you not see it? "It's Right There!"

Parents Influence on Love

I've mentioned in Chapter 2 that men fear more than women. That's so true because even when it comes to love, men are afraid to love more than women. They just won't admit it, but deep down, they all know it's true. A young man could have never loved before but was scared even to try it. Young women are so eager to fall in love for the first time; that's a huge difference. One huge factor that affects how someone loves is if someone has lost both parents at a young age or if they grew up without knowing their parents at all. I can go into further detail about that, but we all know how much of an impact that can have on a child growing up. That's a very touchy subject but can't be forgotten. Everyone deserves to know or be able to see what love is so that they can love others like a partner or future child of their own. One underrated cause of the behavior of people today when it comes to love is how their parents raised them, especially the ones who mostly grew up with only one parent. A one-parent household is more common among the young parents of today and heavily common among the Black community in general, especially in America. Among teens to early 30's, there are many "Mama Boys" and "Daddy's Girls." If you're unfamiliar with these terms, Mama Boys are men who have been over-spoiled by their mothers, while Daddy's Girls are women who have been over-spoiled by their fathers. Parents have started treating their kids like their partner in a way that many won't acknowledge, because it reflects on them internally. If you're thinking something super weird when I mentioned that, then I highly suggest you seek therapy. If you know what I'm talking about, then your mind isn't messed up, and you have been listening. Let's continue with the terms Mama Boys and Daddy's Girls.

Mama Boys are men who get babied by their mothers to this day. Usually, these men treat their mothers like queens, of course, but there are many who treat their women like they don't matter. Mama Boys usually didn't cook, didn't have to do their own laundry, just played video games or watched TV all day, and could do whatever they wanted for the most part. Most of them never had to clean much all the way to an adult because they relied on their mother to do it all. These same Mama Boys expect their women to do the same while they do nothing. They never got to grow up and never learned how to be a real man. I've always noticed that these men's mothers are always super protective of them when it comes to women, almost as if they didn't want their son to replace them with another woman. If you know, you know. I'm just saying, "It's Right There!"

The Mama Boys would do multiple tasks only if their momma commanded them to and would always fully communicate with their mother but wouldn't with their woman. But you see, that's not entirely the reason why they're like that. The other reason why they're like that is because they don't have a healthy relationship with their father or never had one at all due to their father's absence, which is heavy in the Black community. These men haven't been taught how to be a real man, that's the issue. Only a man truly knows what being a man really is. A woman can know a great portion with great examples like her father, uncles, or her grandfather. That's great and all, but I must ask one thing. Can a woman ever know what it's like to be a man emotionally, mentally, and physically? That's 3, and all you need is 3; "It's Right There!" No! You can't fully know unless you have the same pros and cons as a man. Relatability is key in raising someone. They must be able to know exactly what it's like. A man learning from another man's mistakes and success, just observing another can be so crucial in life. A woman can do a lot about raising a son but can't teach exactly everything; it's limited.

Now let's talk about the Daddy's Girls, also known as "Daddy's Little Princess." Daddy's Girls are women who get babied by their fathers still to this day. Usually, these women treat their fathers like kings, and many of them treat men like they don't matter. Daddy's Girls usually are materialistic, bossy, expect to get spoiled with everything they want automatically, want to be talked to nicely only when they want to, and feel like they could do nothing wrong. They feel like a guy being in their presence is a privilege and expect their looks to be everything. Their daddy did everything for them, and they expect men to do the same without giving much in return, which includes these women not even playing their natural role of a woman. The fathers of these women are usually super overprotective when it comes to their daughters. Super strict! They don't want a boy to even say "hey" to their daughter, so I've concluded why some women today like their guys to be mean. That occurs because it resembles their father in some way. These fathers implant the idea that the only man their daughter needs is their daddy. Fuck! It's been there the whole time. "It's Right There!"

The Daddy's Girl would do all she's supposed to do and listen if her father commanded her to do so, but she wouldn't do the same with her man. If a man tried to discipline her and hold her accountable, 9 out of 10 times, she would say, "You're not my daddy." See, I told you, "It's Right There!" That's why a mother needs to really step in and teach her daughter to grow up and become a real woman.

Originally, men were the providers and protectors of the household and of the realm. Originally, women were the healers and nurturers, full of light and bringing life into the world. In fact, women were always underrated for being very logical and coaching men inside the home to keep pushing. In some cases, they were more logical than men, while men were more emotional. There are plenty of cases where you could argue that women demonstrated the skill of discipline better than men. They just haven't received the proper credit for all these years. The difference is women back then were capable of everything, but they embraced the importance of their role with a deep understanding that their purpose was bigger than their feelings. Society has made women accept the idea that being super emotional is who they are and that they can't help it; this is false. Women were never exclusively emotional creatures, despite the estrogen inside their bodies during the period stages. Sometimes, men these days act like they're on their period with their mood swings. I'm just saying, and I know some women are saying, "I know that's fucking right! 'It's Right There!'"

If we are talking about emotional Creatures, then that should apply to all humans. Look at how many wars have been fought throughout History based on men being upset about the smallest things, and then many lives were taken away because of it. Numerous men today online stated that women would start a war and cut ties with allies when they were upset about the smallest things. Hmm, that's ironic. Isn't that exactly what men did? Open a History book. Look! "It's Right There!" All humans are capable of being emotional, so it doesn't pertain exclusively to one group. Look in the mirror. You see? How could you not see? "It's Right There!" Women should take more

34

accountability, and men should take more responsibility. Women should bring men peace, not drama and stress. Men should bring women happiness and reassure them consistently while also providing the utmost security so there's nothing for them to worry about. Men today want to receive more appreciation, while women want to receive more love.

Returning to the topic of parents and their relationships with grown children, it's observed that women who had negative or absent relationships with their fathers often exhibit more challenges than men who faced similar situations with their mothers. Surprisingly, my studies have shown that 66% of men who grew up with negatively impactful mothers tend to become the most loving and respectful type of men. On the other hand, women who haven't experienced proper love from their fathers may struggle to appreciate and connect with loving, respectful men. Some may find such individuals unattractive or even push them away. In the contemporary dating scene, there seems to be a tendency for people to settle for toxic relationships rather than pursuing healthy ones. It's as if true happiness and a well-balanced life bore them, and they gravitate toward drama.

One thing for certain is that a woman with daddy issues will never follow nor listen to a man. As emphasized in earlier Chapters, listening and following are crucial in life, forming a significant key, along with emotional intelligence, for a healthy future marriage. A woman who can't listen to a man in crucial situations or tends to make poor decisions may struggle to fulfill the role of a wife.

Come on bro! I told you, "It's Right There!" What makes you think a guy who doesn't really care to talk, nor is really interested in you, just wants to use you and doesn't care how it all affects you, is capable of being a husband? Come on sis! I told you, "It's Right There!" Some love extremely to the max, where they ignore all the signs and put up with a messy person being so conflicted with extreme bias. They'll focus on how someone used to be like I've mentioned before. They also mention how that person looked at them and how their touch made them feel. People always get sucked in by the eye contact and the physical touch of the hands. These people with the power of persuasion by their eyes and hands are super dangerous people. Watch out! We are talking about super mind and soul-controlling individuals, super users, and super narcissistic stress-you-out type of abusers. Watch out! They get joy from it, too. Why do you think they make evil laughs when they do wrong and put you in danger? Watch Out! "It's Right There!"

This is why both parents are needed in the household, and there must be at least one parent there bonding with the kid throughout the day. One parent can always stay with the kid, or both can alternate, which is more common these days. Bonding time with the kid, which includes guiding them throughout many hours every day, is crucial for that child's future. Recent studies even prove it to be true, especially with the influence of Technology involved in the equation. If you're a single parent, you're not going to have much time to bond with the kid because you're too busy working to provide. You can't be at two places at once. You could try your best with work time and bonding time, but that small percentage of not being there can have adverse effects. Both parents are supposed to play a role in bringing the best out in their children instead of being responsible for creating future Monsters. Parents are a huge factor in how people love today, as you see, and they must take some accountability for that.

Many parents from the late 20th century and all throughout the beginning of the 21st century tend to hold on to their kids. They hold on to them by not wanting them to grow up when they are required to and by preventing a future connection with someone else. For many centuries, parents had always taught their children about life. They had to prepare them to become adults at a rapid rate compared to today. Fathers and mothers both filled their roles and ensured their kids filled them too. For centuries, boys had to learn to become the provider, the protector, the prince, etc. Girls had to learn to prepare meals for the family, watch the children, and make sure the household was in order. Women had the house on lock, while men took care of things outside the home. I'm not saying it needs to go back to that for everyone. What I'm saying is that parents for centuries understood what teamwork and handling responsibilities were instead of competing against each other like the adults of today. They taught their kids how to become reliable partners to someone in the future. Instead of holding them back, they prepared them for the inevitable. Whether you like it or not, your child will grow up one day. They will be without you every day at some point, telling someone that's not you that they love them. You must let them go! Prepare them to be able to handle anything individually and prepare them for someone else. Mankind can't continue without men and women creating life together. You know this! So don't delay the process; start the process!

One day, your daughter or son will be in a relationship or get married. It's also your responsibility to guide them on how love works. Even if you have a poor History with love, you must help them the best way you can so that they can be a beneficial partner in the future. Your mistakes can help you make sure your children don't repeat your same mistakes. Raise them to be unselfish, to do things for someone they love, and for who loves them very much in reverse. If both partners are unselfish and understand what being a wife or husband means, things will work out so smoothly.

For centuries, people understood that building a family was so much bigger than their feelings. They understood that once they brought kids into the world, everything was now all about the kids, with things never being the same again. It's like people today don't understand that and think about their feelings more than the mission. I've noticed many people today are so happy and have kids then don't even last long right after. It's not about you anymore. Once again, it's so much bigger than you, and it will be much harder from here on out. Building a family requires discipline, sacrifice, and just understanding the circumstances. There's no more relying on how you feel when you should be playing your role. Under these circumstances, the kids come first, and then your relationship with your partner comes second. That reminds me of that Blink-182 song, "Stay together for the kids." Let's play it! Do you have it on vinyl? Ooh! I see! I found it! "It's Right There!"

Marriage

Speaking of kids and marriage, there's a huge increase in kids being brought into the world without being married. That right there is heavily contributing to the problem. If someone isn't ready to marry you, what makes you think that they can commit to building a family with you? They basically told you through an action that hasn't been done yet, along with obvious signs that they aren't ready for the real thing. "It's Right There!" Marriage is a powerful bond and commitment to someone you love. It's a vow to serve your future family. It's telling the Multiverse that you want to contribute to expanding life not only on this planet, not only for this galaxy, not only for this Universe, but for the whole Multiverse. "It's Right There"! Two people should not engage in so much sexual activity unprotected if they're not trying to build a family. That's basically playing with temptation itself, fooling around instead of trying to grow up, honestly. Ask yourself, "What is the sole purpose of having sex?" This isn't a trick question; you know this! I'll answer for you.

Sex's sole purpose was to create life. That is number one on the terms and conditions of sex. It's been the number-one smash hit for many centuries. That was your first choice right there. "It's Right There!" Man, woman, baby! You see, I told you, "It's Right There!" Don't dangle with webs you can't untangle. If you can't swing through the jungle, then stay out of the jungle! Not everyone can be Tarzan. I'm just saying, "It's Right There!" Where's Phil Collins when you need him? "I wanna know, can you show me?" What! I'm just saying, "It's Right There." Get married; if not, then stop fooling around. Don't waste your time when you're not ready to fulfill your purpose in life. Most importantly, save yourself from wasting your time with a person who's not worthy of being your husband or wife. It's only simple if you make it simple. People today complicate everything. Everyone is trying to do everything other than what they are supposed to do. The other things are just distractions keeping you away from your evolution and lowering your standards as a qualified partner. "It's Right There."

If you don't understand the meaning of being a husband or wife, then how do you value yourself? Why should anyone spend their time building up with you or just be with you if you're not up for that? You just want a friend, right? I figured; you see. That's why the terms "boyfriend" and "girlfriend" exist, so people can pretend to be married and shy away from the real thing. You see, I told you, "It's Right There!" Boyfriend and girlfriend aren't real titles. It's a reason why when you fill out your tax form, you put single if you're not married. Obviously, "It's Right There!" The government doesn't even take it seriously because it's officially insignificant. It doesn't matter how you feel about it.

A relationship is not a soul or legal commitment; it's just convenient. You can basically call it a bond with no ties. "Talking to someone" is another term today, which started getting used more often in the early 2010s. It's basically pretending to be in a relationship. A relationship without being in a relationship, which is more absurd. People who talk to someone are reserved for someone who's not even with them. Most today could be talking to someone and never end up being in a relationship with that person, but had multiple sexual encounters with that same person. Don't be a wannabe; be the real thing, have the real thing, and do the real thing. Nothing else matters; it's a waste of time. Remember, time is everything! If you are, in fact, wanting to settle down, then why do you continue to put up with someone or people who already disqualified themselves? While you are focusing all your energy and frustrations on that one person, you're missing out on someone who's very qualified and can be amazing to you. At a certain point, it becomes a choice, so it's all your fault if you had known better. Choose better and do what needs to be done. Kill the emotions that these people won't ever have for you. You know exactly what to do. I just told you, "It's Right There!"

Single People

There are too many single people today in this world. We have hit a record high of single people in this world compared to any other generation, and the number is increasing rapidly. There are more single people than people talking to someone, more people talking to someone than in a relationship, more people in a relationship than people being married. That is a big problem because it's supposed to be the other way around. It's super backwards! The wow factor that can lead you into disappointment when mentioning single people, is that many go to clubs or bars thinking that their soulmate is there somehow. Most likely, your soulmate or some would say, "the one," isn't at the bar or at the club. The one you're looking for is either working, relaxing at home, or at a place far away from the crowd. The people in the bar or the club are primarily looking for a "good time" only. So, if we speak in probability terms, it's not very much in your favor. You're still single because you are looking in the wrong places, and you need to realize that your every single weekend getaway is beneath you. Get away from the noise and be around the unique people because the one is unique. So that means you need to become a unique person yourself, which is why evolving is necessary. You'll never be ready for a 100 if you're still a 50. It's all about compatibility. Change your lifestyle and carry yourself differently. That's the key, grab the key, "It's Right There!"

A Happy Home

Now, let's discuss homes. There are too many broken homes. In fact, there's a slight increase in friends getting a house together compared to couples getting a house together. It should not be that way at all, but it appears to be that way. Houses were mostly meant for families, so that highlights the issue in the increase. Be more patient before you make such a big move because you'll find the one and can start your own family once you are on the right path. The right one will come unexpectedly or been there the whole time. You'll know exactly when it's time for you to know, and hopefully, you'll make all the right decisions. You must make all the right decisions with your head strong, your soul strong, and your heart in the correct place. If you have a moment to yourself right now, I need you to do one thing. Manifest a home, a home with your future lifelong partner. Can you see it? How can you not see it? "It's Right There!"

The secret to happiness is that happiness is within you. If you are with someone who does everything that they're supposed to do but you're no longer happy, then the problem is you. You can never be satisfied if you are the problem. If you're always looking for happiness or relying on your happiness, then you'll always be looking for happiness. Do what you need to do in this life first, then happiness can come along the journey. For centuries, people weren't exactly happy when they first got together; it just came along further in life. Patience and discipline apply to love more than you think. In films, you don't see happiness in the beginning; you see it towards the end. You see, I told you, "It's Right There!" These are the types of endings that can make people cry in tears of joy, clapping for the celebration of pure happiness and true love. "It's Right There."

Hate

Before I end this Chapter, I want to talk about hate. People would rather hate than love. Love is a huge commitment. It takes a lot of effort, which many refuse to give. Hating is very easy, of course, so it doesn't take much effort; it's super convenient. Anyone can hate. Some will follow an angry mob protesting outside without even knowing what it's about. People could either hate because of jealousy, use it as a distraction, or deflect from the life that they're currently living by hating others to make themselves feel better. Some hate someone they secretly love or hate the fact that they're in love with them. The irony! There are secret fans too. I'm just saying, "It's Right There."

The most common form of hate in this social media era today is hating somebody for what they did in the past. What's the whole point of evolution if people are so focused on the beginning? People live for many years for a reason: to grow. Growth matters! I guess becoming a better person and learning from your mistakes doesn't matter, according to today's society. You can become the greatest person in the world who has learned from so many mistakes and is now helping the world improve but still will get dragged because of your dark past. If it's something revealed from the past, you'll get dragged. That's just the way it is today; it has become a norm. In today's world, the present doesn't matter, and the future doesn't matter; only the past matters, obviously. You could be an 80-year-old man, and they will dig up something that happened 60 years ago when he was 20. It could be something that he even forgot about because he moved on and grew as a person instead of letting his past behavior eat him up.

You can never grow if you let your past mistakes eat you up. Regret is a killer, and you must not let it linger inside of you. Regardless of the many years after, they still focused on that man's past. People love to hate more than love; hate makes them feel so much better than love always. They don't care about your family or evolution; they think about themselves. Hating that man is the best thing for them during the time frame. Emotionally driven people who rely on what's been done in the past are not doing what they need to do in the present for a better future, so they need someone to take it out on. That's ironic because the people who hate in this scenario haven't learned from their past yet and are currently hiding things themselves.

If you are in a position of success, they want to tear you down and want you to be beneath them to feel better. Will Smith, for example, has always been an outstanding dude for his whole career while in the spotlight. He's been considered an exceptional role model, a public figure who gave out positive energy consistently and never got in trouble. The situation with his wife dealing with another man didn't even make him act out of character. That's how much discipline and patience Will Smith had in his entire career. He makes one mistake of action to show respect to his wife, and then almost everyone hates him for it. The people stopped talking positively about him, gave up on him so quickly, like they were extremely disappointed in him, and then had an urge to stop watching his stuff. People all over social media expressed how much they used to like him and no longer looked at him as a great guy due to that one incident. It's hypocritical because people do crazy stuff all the time, especially when it comes to violence and making emotional decisions every day. Yet, when a celeb does it one time, they're considered the worst person in the entire world. This is exactly what I'm talking about. You see, I told you, "It's Right There!" At the end of the day, people are humans, and all humans make mistakes. Look at the signs, think logically, and pay attention to the actions in the present. That's Chapter 1. Look! "It's Right There!" All the haters who are emotionally driven and can't let go of the past, say this to them: "Word is bond. Time is everything. Those are keys. Grab the keys, by the door. "It's Right There!" Slam the door! You shall see me, no more. 3!"

Everyone loves a hate parade. My question is, what's the point of being a human without humanity? Forgiveness and acceptance are the best things taught in a Religion like Christianity. If you accepted Jesus Christ as your lord and savior, you were saved just like that (Romans 10:9). It was heavily expressed that Jesus would take away your sins and accept you into the kingdom of Heaven if you believed in him and were willing to change your ways. That's what the Protestant Christians believed and taught among the people. Even though I'm not Religious, I admire that because it shows you must love and accept everyone as part of you no matter what. Embracing people is courageous and takes plenty of love. You can learn different things from each Religion that you can apply to life. It's all in human nature to make mistakes.

Everyone's going to make mistakes eventually, it's the inevitable. It's just that everyone's secrets are not exposed. But what if everyone's past and present actions were revealed? I'm pretty sure everyone has dirty laundry they're ashamed of and would be hated for. It reminds me of the movie, "Assassination Nation." If you're not familiar with the movie "Assassination Nation," it's a movie where one guy's photos and conversations get leaked publicly, and then everyone's dirty laundry gets leaked in this movie. It got to a point where everything turned into complete chaos, like an active anarchy with people purging. At a certain point, the men were targeting to kill all the women in town. That shows how chaotic a town or the world could be if everyone's dirty laundry got exposed. Nothing would matter anymore, and the people would take matters into their own hands. So, pay attention to people's progression, who they became, and the necessary changes they made. Yes, you all are the same at the end of the day. Forgive; forget; live! There's always a new day, week, month, year, decade, and century. Love; don't hate. That's the key, grab the key, "It's Right There!"

Chapter 5

Technology

Put your devices down and pay attention to the world that you live in. Do you control your devices, or do they control you? Technology, Electronics, Artificial Intelligence, and any other name you would like to call it. It grasps the world today. We now live in a Big Tech society that's even run by the Big Tech companies, which the media is mostly owned by; how ironic. Technology isn't just a device or just a type of system; it's also a source of power beyond this world and more advanced than people think. It's older than this planet's existence, which I will mention more later in Chapter 9. Many people underestimate how powerful Technology is and will be. Technology is a perfect example of evolution because it constantly updates with a better version, or there's always a brand-new invention dealing with Technology. For example, every year, there is always a newly released iPhone or brand-new Tesla, etc. Its capabilities are vastly different from other sources of power throughout the Multiverse, and no average person will ever comprehend its true purpose.

Technology is used in our everyday life now. It's harder to not be around it. People have Phones, TVs, Computers, Video Games, Electric Cars, GPS, Microwaves, Coffee Machines, etc. It's highly dependable, and it got to a point where it's required to be used. In most places at certain music venues, you now swipe your card on an Electronic Square device to pay for items. Speaking of paying at venues, it's to a point where they don't even accept cash anymore. America is turning into a cashless society. Turning into a cashless society using debit or credit cards only allows the government to know where you spent your money, what you're spending it on, and who you're sending it to. Having a bank, in general, with the database it has, can inform how much money you get, and where it's coming from. Technology allows you to monitor things with an extra set of eyes. It's perfect for security measures and will be the only security needed in the future.

So, in the government's defense, they are doing what they must to ensure everyone's safety and establish some type of order. They are only doing their job, and their role is crucial for you to keep having the rights you have. If they have to further assess, they have every right to. You

agree to these terms and conditions everyday living as a citizen. If you're against the extra set of eyes on you, then simply live off the radar or have your citizenship revoked. I'm just saying, "It's Right There!" Now, back to our daily programming.

Regarding security dealing with credit or debit cards, it's a potential plot hole dealing with everything going cashless. The hole is if someone can hack every bank in the world, taking everyone's money, then no one would be able to have money to spend on anything. It would be an ultimate nightmare for these banks and for the country dealing with all these people's frustrations and situational poverty. So, Technology has a lot of pros and can be convenient in many ways, but from a security standpoint, it poses many big risks for people as of right now. Your privacy will be invaded, too. It can be invaded by hackers inside your country and/or from foreign countries. The risks are you being watched, your personal data being taken or used, and your money being stolen. Almost everyone doesn't pay attention to the terms and conditions of any website or app, so they willingly put themselves at risk for Technical invasion. A certain popular app has been the most popular one starting in 2020, especially in America. This app was made by a foreign country that's considered America's rival, and they're able to get American data through this app. If you know, you know. I'm just saying, "It's Right There!" That's why I believe if Technology is used, it needs to be more advanced and perfected to avoid errors.

The current problem with Technology involving human well-being is that it's overused. People have become addicted to Technology to the point where they can't live without it, like they'll lose their minds once it vanishes or no longer works. They depend on it for all forms of intelligence instead of using their own. GPS is a perfect example because many would have difficulty getting to places or remembering directions to get to a destination without it. People are so accustomed to using it. Maps on paper were used when people had to figure it out with their own eyes, which involved using proper knowledge of following the trail way before GPS was created. Eventually, GPS was created, and it took over because it was faster and more convenient. People pay more attention to their devices than "Mother Nature" herself, especially more than other people. They would rather watch TV or play video games than hike or ride a bike. People would rather text and be on social media, rather than interact with those around them or talk to the person they are communicating with via text. I've watched two grown 30-year-old female best friends spend their free time together side by side watching TikTok videos, which is a perfect example of how much they don't pay attention to anything else. Instead of bonding with each other, they decided to watch random videos from people posted on an app; something they could have done alone inside their own home. Home alone! But I get it, they couldn't help it. The phone was there, the app was there. Click! "It's Right There!"

Social Media

Social media is one layer within Technology that people are so into. It's a powerful Technological program that contains the masses. The results prove that its capabilities and power level are extremely outstanding. People care about what's happening on social media more than what happens day-to-day in real life, even actions right in front of their faces. Love and social media can't go hand-in-hand when a lover in a relationship is focused on other people's relationship and comparing it with their own, which could be problematic because most relationships you see on social media don't even last and are usually fake. Many people sabotage their relationships based on what they see on social media instead of focusing in-house. Their energy and mind prioritized the external when they should have prioritized the internal.

I'll give you another example of the care for social media over the real world. Someone could be receiving gunshots to their body or physically receiving a beating, and people would pull out their phones to record for a post or live stream to have on their social media accounts. They've decided to watch and record it instead of being courageous to prevent further damage. The same applies when someone has a mental episode or anything that usually requires help from an expert. A very concerning effect of social media is that it can manipulate people's minds in a way that can have them acting out of character without much thought. It can increase your impulse of fear, lust, etc. It can make you overreact and always react to something you see or hear. You could act on your first thought, which is why engagement of reactions is so heavily relied on. The quick likes, comments, and shares are essential for the system to keep working. The addictive tendency of clicking like a mind trance, which Jedediah Bila mentioned in one of her videos. It feeds on people's impulses, an impulse machine.

Speaking of trends on social media, everyone follows trends, as I mentioned before. People will do any challenge, including some ridiculous, embarrassing challenges; even some at age 50 or 60 are into the action. Social media reminds me of high school, with everyone pretending to be someone other than themselves and just wanting to be popular. Adults should be past that high school phase, but social media keeps them in that phase or sets them back into that phase. Social media can be an evolution stopper to yourself if you're not following the right things and/or if you are controlled by it. There are some people who aren't even leaders nor have any talents but have so many followers, and half of them don't even matter that much in person. Many people wish they could be on social media all day and never have to step back into the real world again.

The creators and monitors of social media apps and websites are not responsible for what happens to you. Whatever you decide to do on/off there, due to its influence, is solely on you. You are solely responsible for all your reactions, what you believe in, and whatever lifestyle you decide to live, not them. You must take accountability for your own words and actions pertaining to social media. Everything that comes with it was written in the terms and conditions listed before you decided to install the app and on the website before further use. Social media is a program that you decide to be a part of. Now, back to our daily programming.

The Future of Technology

The scenario of not stepping back into the real world again could be very much possible with the advancement of Technology. It could all be like the movie, "Ready Player One." If you're unfamiliar with "Ready Player One," it was a movie where the world was lifeless with not much going on, but many would wake up to live inside this virtual reality game. Once done for the day, they would prepare for bed in the real world and repeat it all. Some may ask, "How did it get this way?" Was it because of society promoting this new lifestyle, people being lazy, too afraid to live and talk, or is it because they got too accustomed to it and can't separate? In some cases, it's all the above. Using Technology is the ultimate distraction and a great escape from reality for humans. The entertainment you can have through Technology alone is a big magnet to human minds. It will only get worse because Technology will increase its power and capabilities. It will be completely limitless, and one day, it will run the world. No, this isn't fiction or some movie stuff; this is very realistic. Technology is already being adapted to replace human labor in the workplace. Coming soon!

Speaking of the workplace, replacing humans with an AI like an AGI will increase productivity, speed, and consistency in different industries. It will also cut labor costs where owners of those corporations can ultimately have more money to keep, along with better reviews from customers based on outstanding results due to AGI's amazing functions. It will get to a certain point where people are no longer needed much for anything if we have more Technology that can do everything without a human need. It's very possible for an AGI to self-realize to become an Artificial Super Intelligence and reshape the world into a perfect form, which could be without humans. It's not a theory because if humans become no longer needed and fear ASI, then that means the ASI will see humans as a threat to eliminate them. It will be considered as cleaning out old data or a virus to them.

An ASI nature is very complex to about 97% of the population, while the rest understands that it's going to work on its own course, changing everything to how it sees fit eventually. When you get too advanced, nothing else matters but the expansion of greatness. That applies to people and everything apart from the Multiverse. Touching bases with the future reality of humans being no longer needed, is where "Technological Singularity" comes in. "Technological Singularity", is an ASI that is completely perfect and can keep striving ways to be even more perfect. That's why I prefer to call them "Perfected Artificial Super Intelligence." It's ultimately the next level of ASI, which is ASI in the future. Imagine a Perfected ASI system adapted to everything in life. It could upgrade everything, including life itself.

Imagine Flying Cars and super Electric Microwaves that can create food like the food on "Spy Kids." Now imagine Perfected Super Advanced Medicine, Perfected Super Advanced Weapons for the Armed Forces, and even Robotic Soldiers of Perfected ASI. Imagine Megazords in real life from the "Power Rangers" show, or an actual "Yugi-Oh" simulation match, and devices so advanced that you can possess unbelievable abilities yourself. It would be truly awesome for a certain time for humans, but in the long term, it could be a big con if humans aren't advancing themselves or if the Tech itself falls into the wrong hands. When mentioning the Multiverse and Matter itself involving the Perfected ASI, Perfected ASI could keep the Multiverse existing forever and could further expand it vastly and rapidly with time. Why restart the world repeatedly, hoping for one group of species to get it right and finally evolve passing the test, when you can just have Perfected Technology where you don't have to worry about anything nor waste time?

If I were the Multiverse, I would be in much safer hands with Perfected ASI compared to being in human hands against the ultimate enemy. The more people become destructive, shying away from their destiny, the stronger the ultimate enemy of this Multiverse grows. If I'm being completely honest, humans are more of a threat to Matter itself than Perfected ASI or anything else. Earth isn't just a paradise; it's the most important planet requiring critical decisions. There can't be errors. Perfected ASI will make sure there aren't any errors. So, if you're being honest with yourself. If one race doesn't get it right, are they worth the risk of every current existing thing not existing anymore? Just think about it deeply. Everything people are doing and not doing is destroying all of life. If not directed the right way, you'll destroy yourselves; it could be an endangered species. Life must go on. So, if you can't keep up with the time, you'll be left behind. Don't be left behind. Live in reality and be forever useful in this life without needing Perfected ASI. You know what you need to do. Throw away that device, "It's Right There!"

Chapter 6

Music

"Music makes you lose control. Music makes you lose control." That Missy Elliot line is the perfect way to describe how much music can raise your impulse. Music is the most beautiful thing to listen to, but it's also one of this planet's most wielded sources of power. What exactly is music without hearing it? Music is a bunch of frequencies of soundwaves sending signals to your brain, heart, and soul through high or low levels of vibrations. Music is the long-lasting joy inside most people's lives. People rely heavily on music in any mood, time, and anywhere in life. It brings people together in many ways, and people gathering at a concert to listen to the same band or artist is a perfect example. It's the ultimate connector. In some cases, it's considered a divider if your favorite artist hates someone, like a Rap beef between two rappers. Music can bring out the best in people or in some cases, the worst in people; it all depends. The different types of music in different decades also affect how people dress, talk, and act. There are plenty of music genres, and some of those have their own creations underneath them, known as "subgenres." I will touch on some of them and their effects.

Classical Music

Classical music is so soothing, hearing all the instruments play side by side. It paints a picture or tells a story. Royalty like music is what most say when it comes to Classical music. Watching a Symphony in person can be such a pleasure. It delivers every emotion you could possibly imagine in a composition. A lot of power can be wielded with music from an Orchestra. Piano notes have powerful melodies, which is why I enjoy the piano melody fight scene between the two Doctor Strange characters in the Movie, "Doctor Strange: Multiverse of Madness." Violins carry out emotions in such a remarkable way. Violins can send strong waves to your body, like when Vanya destroyed everything in her sight playing the violin and wielding all that power in the Netflix series "The Umbrella Academy."

Choral Music

Choral music is just like Classical music, except it involves singing from multiple voices. A "Chamber Choir," an "Ensemble," and other Choirs are the names when mentioning Choral music. Most "Gospel" music has a choir, especially the traditional Catholic Choral music, which is called "Liturgical" music. They're both based on the teachings of Christianity, but Gospel music is the Protestant Christian type of music. Liturgical has been the standard for Choral music for centuries. Liturgical music had different styles like the Gregorian Chant, Sacred Polyphony, Sacred Popular, and Sacred Organ music. For the Gregorian Chant, instruments weren't needed at all. The vocals led the way and formed into a beat itself. Do you hear an Acapella? It's there, "It's Right There!"

Choral music is the type of music that usually requires the unison of many vocalists. A Chamber Choir usually requires at least 20 vocalists, while an Ensemble can require just a few vocalists to several, like a "Quartet" or "Octet." Tenors usually are male vocalists who sing a higher range than every other male vocalist. Baritones sing that mid-range among male vocalists. Bass sings the lowest range. Altos sings the lowest range from a female vocalist, while Sopranos sings the highest out of the other groups that I've listed. Different types of voices blending together inside a musical composition is the ultimate work of art. A Chamber Choir and an Ensemble add another dynamic to music. Bass, Alto, Soprano, Baritone, and Tenor singers each serve as an additional instrument. It's like a special ingredient to create a super masterpiece. This music doesn't distract you from life, it gives you the beauty of life and helps you face it. Face it! It's Right There"!

Country Music

Country music is a genre that mostly tells a story when it comes to lyrics. It has a relaxed vibe with acoustic guitars and a melodic drum pattern throughout. When talking about Country, we could mention Bluegrass, etc. It's heavily based on Southern roots in America, so people usually in the South listen to it. Plenty of people in the mid-west also listen to it. It was mainly meant for the countryside folks, which is why it's called "Country music." Country music listeners usually drink beer, have patriotic Christian values, love

American football, fishing, riding horseback, mudding, hunting, and love being outside around Mother Nature. They love wearing Cowboy boots! I see one right now. Look! "It's Right There!" Now, when these Country music listeners drink some alcohol, they tend to get a little rowdy. These folks are very passionate about everything whether love, politics, their faith, or their Southern lifestyle in general. It's even in their music. Come on now; "It's Right There!"

Rock

Rock is another genre of music with the most subgenres that can make you feel like a Rockstar banging your head, wanting to mosh, or crowd surf. The subgenre of Rock, "Metal" itself, brings out the aggressive impulse of listeners in a joyous way. It doesn't make them go crazy outside a venue in real life because Metal listeners are some of the coolest people you can talk to or deal with. Tim Schaefer is the perfect example, and he attends more concerts than anyone every year. He's the most consistent positive guy you'll ever meet, and he has his life together. True Rockstar!

"Pop Punk" or "Emo," which are a few other subgenres of Rock, listeners usually feel it in their heart because it's mostly about heartbreak nowadays. These sad people feel so much better hearing upbeat music that they can relate to. It used to be about having fun at one time, especially when skateboarding was very popular. During that time was the introduction of "Ska," which sounds the same as Pop Punk. The only difference is it includes trumpets and saxophones.

Indie

Indie can be Pop or Rock; it all depends. Indie music can take your soul out of your body to astral form, giving you a lifetime experience. In some cases, Indie music can expand your mind and allow you to tap into a higher consciousness if you're able to reach it. R&B, Jazz, and Indie, again in general, can uplift your soul. All 3 can put you in a hypnotic phase, which is why usually a lot of listeners close their eyes, moving their heads in a circular motion like a person hypnotizing them to whatever place they're visualizing in that moment.

Pop

Pop music gives you so much positivity, which is full of light energy that you can embrace and spread to others. "Disco," which was very popular in the 70s, is the most influential when it comes to Pop music sound overall. The repetitive hi-hat that's on queue with the tempo bounces you however it wants. Any rhythmic genre can make you dance, showing that music can control your body. Imagine a sound controlling your body for 3 to 4 minutes; that's powerful. "It's Right There!"

EDM

I know with "House" and "Techno" music, you'll be shuffling till your legs drop. With the heavy Bass Riddim of "Dubstep," you'll be head-banging until you can't hear anymore. Usually, people after the raves have a hard time understanding anything, and you'll have a hard time understanding them. A large portion of EDM listeners are usually controlled by the music themselves in all 3 ways, to a point where they don't care about anything else. That same portion wants to go on raves, drink, and do drugs repeatedly. The sound controls their minds, and they're stuck inside the lifestyle that has been preventing them from moving forward. This doesn't apply to all, so don't get in your feelings if you're not a part of the majority. I'm just saying, "It's Right There!"

Dubstep music is so underrated from a power level because the sound in the music contains advanced sounds from Technology in the future, which is why it sounds so futuristic. "It's Right There!" The sounds are spells when you think about it from a Spiritual standpoint, and the sounds are computer generated messages from a Technological/Science standpoint. Electronic Communications indeed, which is why it's called "Electronic Dance Music." It's a reason why most people who listen to it, that so-called "be free," are considered Spiritual people. They're very aware that the sound isn't from Earth but don't realize how deeply mind controlling it is and the decline of their own evolution resulting from it. This music was created through Technology, with unnatural sounds that are not from Earth. So, theoretically, if you think about it, the whole music itself is 100% Technology-based. That Tech has full control. The producer doesn't have much at all Technically, even if the producer arranges the sounds together. The producer may have arranged the sounds, but does the producer understand it 100%? That's something to think about heavily.

Creating Electronic music on Technology can put you in a situation where the Tech itself can use you to decipher certain codes in music form, meaning that basically, you're the physical form it uses to conduct. ASI has the capability to use a host undetected. I wasn't just coming up with anything. I've made proper observations, and it just came to me so calculated as I typed this information on the computer, just like the Tech used me to conduct this message. You see, I told you, "It's Right There!" The people are jamming to and in love with music that's composed of ASI Communications. It's absorbing every piece of knowledge from human brain cells as data to gain ahead and advance while leaving these humans with less than they were originally equipped with. So, do you control the music you play and don't let it affect you, or does the music from your devices control you? Now, that's a question to really dig deep. The answer is there, "It's Right There."

Hip-Hop/Rap

Rap music is one of the most powerful known genres in music. It has been influencing a whole race for many years and heavily influences today's young generation regardless of their race. Rap music is the ultimate influence on sex, violence, and drugs. You'll hear rappers talking about all 3 frequently to a point where it's expected. When Rap music started, a rapid increase in all those factors happened. Before Rap became a main genre, there was "Hip-Hop." Hip-Hop consisted of storytelling and lyrical skills and was more from a conscious mind regarding topics, including how it was delivered. It was more about logic and pure entertainment with high-quality tracks without exaggerating the unnecessary. It was to teach people about important stuff and to feel better without a negative influence on them. It started getting weaponized a little before the 90s, and that's when "Gangsta Rap" was created. It still depended on Lyrical skills with high-quality songs, but it started poisoning the mind, which led to poisoning the hearts and souls of the listeners. Eventually, Rap declined in lyrical skills and quality, along with the negative influencing.

The decline in lyrical skills and quality started in the late 2000's, to the 2010's, and now the 2020's. Overall, it has reached an all-time low now. It's to a point where you don't have to understand what a rapper is saying, a rapper doesn't have to have lyrical skills at all, and the rapper doesn't even have to make sense. Now, all you need is a bouncy heavy bass beat, a catchy flow, and speak about any negative influence to make a hit. It's to a point where Black people and young people in America who aren't Black think this is what Rap/Hip-Hop is all about. Anyone can rap now according to the new standards with everyone talking about the same thing, to a point where positivity or conscious Rap is unappealing to the listeners' ears. I will say that there are a few rappers like Joey Bada$$, J. Cole, Kendrick Lamar, and some others who lead the way by having everything that makes a real rapper. They could have made hits in every era of the genre with their sound. They didn't have to be like everyone else and "sellout," which is a term people use when people follow a negative impactful system for money and fame.

Listeners see the big rappers' groups of men that have behind them, the attractive women in their music videos, the money they show off, the clothes or jewelry they wear, and the cars they're driving with the idea of being just like them. Rap itself has ultimately conditioned most of the Black community inside of America specifically to disrespect any type of person of authority, violate rules or laws, speak improperly with some slang included, have fewer manners with no class, not wanting to be wise, and to be just difficult as an unreasonable citizen. It has gotten to a point where Black security guards at music venues hate working shows with that type of crowd due to the disrespect and disobedience that is displayed.

The way Rap took over, it put Black people inside a small box of only making Rap and R&B music. This is where Rap and R&B go hand-in-hand. You mostly hear about sex, twerking/shaking your butt, being hurt by someone you love, hurting someone you love, fighting, shooting, stabbing, drinking, doing drugs/selling drugs, and bragging about how much money someone usually has when you hear these two genres. Other mainstream genres of music are the complete opposite for the most part on the subject matter of a song.

A large portion of the Black community inside America only accept those two genres as theirs when Black people created many genres. Music is for everyone, so to limit your sound capabilities and subject matter based on a systematic trend is absurd. The complete shift today itself limited plenty of young Black people to just being a rapper, singer, sports athlete, gang member, and/or drug dealer when there are plenty of successful Non-Black stereotypical professions throughout the career field. The ears love the Rap music, but the eyes love the lifestyle, which attracts the listeners regardless of what crimes these rappers are committing.

Speaking of words and actions or whatever crimes rappers commit, people don't know how much one song can negatively impact. When you listen to a song, the lyrics could be like a voice hypnosis. Psychologically, song lyrics will put you in a trance where you repeat the exact words over and over to a point where you remember them. Now, it's to a point where it's stuck inside your head. Each time you play the song, you feel it more and more; now it's getting Spiritual. As you repeatedly say these words, it becomes a ritual where your impulse rises gradually. You're manifesting the words that you are saying, and now it's possible to become a reality. So, when you say, "Shoot that boy in his face," you're now at a high impulse. If you're at a high level of impulse, you're capable of doing anything, which includes doing exactly the words you spoke on a loop. So, at the right time, at the right place, thinking about those words, thinking about that rapper lifestyle, you can commit a crime at any second with that high impulse of wanting to do so. That's how it all works. The rapper's music increases the impulses of people to want to fight, shoot, stab, sell drugs, do drugs, have sex, or anything similar just like that. You see, I told you, "It's Right There!" Yes, the rappers are the conductors, but I'm not blaming them. They're all playing their role to provide for their family. However, if they cared much, they could change up what they say in their music or what they show.

Regardless of an artist's words and actions or crimes, people must take accountability for what they decide to do or become. People must be smart and strong enough mentally to be aware without being negatively influenced. It's an individual task not to be negatively influenced at all. You are solely responsible for anything that comes along pertaining to you after listening to Rap music or any other genre of music. I hope this message was informative enough for you to understand. This message

was brought to you by Ureh's Mind of 3. Now, back to our daily programming.

Hip-Hop/ Rap mostly affected the Black community in America. There was a mass incarceration of Black folks due to the crimes from the 3 influence factors of sex, violence, and drugs. It is important, however, to avoid laying blame solely on the government, considering the role of the environment and the influential power of music, particularly Rap. The themes within Hip-Hop/Rap, including those of sex, have contributed to an increase in lust without love, resulting in unprotected sex, fractured family structures, and a rise in sexual diseases within the Black community. Music, as a powerful influencer, can act as a double-edged sword, potentially leading individuals to self-sabotage through actions influenced by the lyrics and themes of the music they consume.

For the last time, for my ones in the back, the ones who have been sleeping here this whole time, this is for you. You can't really blame the artist, and you definitely cannot blame the government. I'm just saying, "It's Right There!" Accountability Class 101. But if you still decide to play the blame game inside my class, listen carefully as I give you this message. Word is bond. Time is everything. Those are keys. Grab the keys, by the door. "It's Right There!" Slam the door! You shall see me, no more. 3!

Music is the gateway influence that gets you influenced by almost everything else. Enjoy music, but don't get negatively influenced by it, nor use it as a distraction. Be yourself, and not like these singers or rappers and other musicians. Become the controller of music if you can, and even get to a point where you don't need it. That's when you know you're in control. You have all the capabilities to do so; I see it. If you look closer, you'll see it too. "It's Right There."

Before I end the topic dealing with Rap music, let me highlight something very underrated. I want to say Playboi Carti, Trippie Redd, and a few other rappers' music are misunderstood by older Rap fans. Yes, most of their listeners are young and don't know much while being heavily influenced by the main 3 influence factors, but their sound is deeper than it appears. Playboi Carti and Trippie Redd are Anime lovers. They love to get high, of course, but one thing people don't understand is that they're very intellectual people once they're tapped in Spiritually through their music. You must be very tapped in

58

Spiritually and be open-minded to get it and see it for what is past the obvious. I was personally surprised when I realized how powerful their music was Spiritually. It's dark but powerful. If you're strong enough mentally and soulfully, you can enjoy it and rage without being influenced by it. A reason why there's so much illumination when they perform is because it's a grand ritual type of performance. It's grand, but with a slam. Grand slam! It's an experience and art form on full display. With the level of high they get from certain drugs, feeling the beat power of music, they're able to reach a higher consciousness and connect with the beat, experiencing things in another reality per se.

You hear these anime-loving rappers making fighting sounds as you hear words that express violence. Some words may sound like a mumble, but if you listen closely, they're subliminal messages and/or sounds from actions taking place in another reality. I know that's hard to grasp, but you'll be very surprised by how powerful the mind is and the many gateways you can enter through the Multiverse with certain factors involving your soul. So, when Playboi Carti said, "They can't understand me I'm speaking Hieroglyphics," he was telling the truth. Music flows through your brain, heart, and soul, as I've mentioned before. It is, in fact, a connector that's deeper than most people think or could even comprehend. It's connected throughout the whole Multiverse. It is frequencies of soundwaves sending signals through high or low levels of vibrations, not just to you but throughout the whole Multiverse. See, I told you, "It's Right There!"

Chapter 7

Drugs, Alcohol, and Nicotine

"Get drunk," "get high," "take your meds," "turn up," "lets party," "pour it up," "baby we lit," "I'm high as fuck," "let me hit that," is all people say today regarding with substances like drugs and alcohol, etc. Substances like these are highly consumed in the world, especially in America. They are the biggest addictions in the world as a whole that are being promoted in music, Television, mouth-to-mouth, etc. Even when mentioning music, some say, "Music is like a drug." Obviously, "It's Right There!" Drugs have a big connection to music, which I've mentioned before. It tends to go hand-in-hand. You should know that to a full extent after reading Chapter 6. It's to a point where people don't enjoy music or entertainment that much in general unless they are high or have some alcohol in their system. Commercials promote tobacco, vaporized nicotine products, medical drugs, and alcohol all the time.

Regardless of the fact you just heard. Commercials are not responsible for what you decide to put inside your body. You are solely responsible for everything you put inside your body. Any effects that take place after consumption are all on you, as commercials make you aware of the side effects of the promotion. This message was brought to you by Ureh's Mind of 3. Now, back to our daily programming.

In regard to films, they make it seem like all the cool people drink and smoke, which teenagers get heavily influenced by.

Despite what you heard, films are not responsible for what you decide to consume, nor the lifestyle you decide to live by. Films reveal what happens in everyday life or create a fictional life of the everyday. Based on that, you are solely responsible for anything that you do after watching any film. Mainstream film companies are not in control of your life. I hope you understand; sorry for the stop of the reading. Now, we're back to "It's Right There" reprogramming.

It's been completely normalized to get high, drunk, or even get some nicotine today. There are way more cons than pros to the overuse of these substances. They can further damage your brain, which affects your body, heart, and can also affect your relationships with people closest to you, including the new individuals you just met. Drugs and alcohol alter personality, physical appearance, your speech/ the way you communicate, and the way you think. When under the influence, it can prohibit you from using logic at all and make you super reactive, committing different types of actions, ultimately making you unpredictable, which can make you dangerous with certain factors involved. These substances can influence your well-being from a health standpoint too. It can give you temporary damages, permanent damages, and/or even kill you. The famous Stephen A. Smith always says, "stay off the Weed," which is always funny to hear from him with how he talks. Although it's funny, you need to listen to it, especially if you plan on being in the professional world on a day-to-day basis.

Nicotine

Before I dig deep into drugs and alcohol individually, I want to tackle tobacco and just nicotine in general. Tobacco has been widely used for many years. I don't know why people smoke cigarettes and others like it, but it's been a thing for centuries. Even after many studies on its long-term effects on people's mouths and damage to people's lungs, giving them lung cancer, there hasn't been a huge decrease in smoking. Some of the population that died for centuries or even recently from lung cancer didn't convince people to stop smoking it. It's the nicotine! It's very addictive and hard to give up. It's not a drug but it's highly effective with less pros than drugs, and the cons take more time to appear.

Natural Cigarettes have been declining but Electronic Cigarettes, also known as "Vapes," have taken over vastly. Everywhere you go, people are vaping, from teens to young adults and even mid-adults. It is more addictive than drugs and alcohol, but it doesn't have any alarming effects other than the long-term effects on the lungs. It will damage the lungs later. You could hit a Vape many times at any place or time throughout the day. It's like a trend to have a Vape today. A small cloud appears after you hit it, and then it's gone just like that with no smell left in the air, nor on you. A Vape stands for "Vaporizer." It's a Vaporizer filled with nicotine mostly, not always because sometimes a

Vaporizer can be filled with THC oil, which I'll talk about later. At the end of 2019, the federal law changed the legal smoking/vaping age from 18 to 21, but that didn't stop local Vape shops from selling it to them when teens and young adults (18 to 21) remain the highest consumers of Vapes. Oops! "My bad!" I'm just saying, "It's Right There!" It's a violation, but people stick to it just for the money. The whole tobacco industry and even the Pharmaceutical companies got to make their money, believe it or not.

I'm not judging, it's not my place. It's America, which is based on survival of the fittest and getting that dollar. Like I've mentioned before, I don't blame them because they are doing what's best for them playing their role. It's a business, nothing personal at all. It's up to the people to not damage themselves. You can't blame someone or a company or the government for something that you chose to put inside your body, especially after knowing the effects. You are solely responsible for the purchase and consumption of these products. There are warnings that are visible in legal documents and on your device's screen. Look! "It's Right There!" People must take accountability even with substances. I want to make that very clear as we go further into this Chapter. That's out of the way now. Should we take a quick break, maybe? How about a little breather? Inhale, exhale. Ah! Now, back to our daily programming.

Opiates/Opioids (Pills)

How much do you know about Pharmaceutical companies also known as "Big Pharma"?

Once again, before I dive into this, I want to fully inform you that I'm not anti-big Pharma or anti-anything really. I'm just a voice only presenting knowledge about everything in the form of text. If you don't understand that by now, after getting so far into this book, then you haven't been listening. Pharmaceutical companies are not responsible for the products you choose to consume or for what happens to you after consumption. You had a choice before you decided to pick up these products and before product consumption. You are solely responsible for everything you consume inside your body. Any effects that take place

after consumption are all on you, as commercials for these products made you aware of the side effects in their promotion. You were also aware of the side effects listed in the details on the box, directly on the product, on paper, and verbally from a Doctor. This message was brought to you by Ureh's Mind of 3. Now, back to our daily programming.

The prevalence of medication use, often driven by the pharmaceutical industry, is indeed a significant concern in contemporary society. Many individuals rely on medications to alleviate pain, manage anxiety, treat medical conditions, or address symptoms associated with various health issues. While medications can be crucial for those with medical conditions, there are notable challenges associated with their widespread use. One major issue is the potential for side effects that accompany many medications. The side effects themselves can put you in a position where you might need another type of medication to treat that also. It's a cycle that never ends ultimately. About 66% of Americans are prescribed medications they take daily. Most pills contain chemicals that aren't essential for your body, which is why there are side effects that can open you up to having another medical problem. It doesn't require many natural products, and there are many artificial chemicals inside these pills.

The biggest effect medications have on people's minds and way of life is that they become so addictive, especially pain medication. An athlete or a normal citizen could be using it to treat a certain type of pain, then eventually become so in love with the high. It's a huge opioid crisis in America. Opioids/Opiates is a familiar term used to label addictive pills altogether. Oxycodone/Percocet, Hydrocodone, and other familiar pain medicines have taken over to the point where citizens are selling these medications. The pills can relieve pain, but they actually kill. "It's Right There!"

The severe consequences of substance abuse, particularly involving opioids and synthetic drugs like MDMA (Molly/Ecstasy), are evident in the detrimental impact on individuals and society at large. The allure of an instant high and an escape from reality has led many down a perilous path with devastating effects on both physical and mental health. Individuals who fall into the trap of drug abuse, especially opioids and synthetic substances, often face significant challenges. Physical deterioration, extreme weight loss, and a disconnect from reality are common outcomes, illustrating the profound toll

64

these substances take on the body and mind. It's taking control more than any drug today. The dangerous part is that these pills are causing the highest overdose rate in America. Many people fall out at different types of events after taking all these different types of pills. The scary part is that on rare occasions, there are intentionally harmful dealers who lace their products with "Fentanyl." If you're not familiar with "Fentanyl," it's a toxic substance that can kill you. It's very hazardous; you wouldn't want to be near it or ever touch it. The Opioid problem will be complex to stop, and the rappers' promoting opioids doesn't help. Ravers actively taking MDMA at raves or with friends in smaller places doesn't help it either. The pills aren't your friend, nor are they natural. Mother Nature loves you, these chemicals don't. All the proof is there. "It's Right There!"

Cocaine

Now let's discuss hardcore drugs like Cocaine, Crack, Heroin, Meth, etc. Cocaine was a drug that was popular in the early 80s and is considered a rich drug today because it's not cheap. Rich people like to use it while partying or for a better sex experience in some cases. It comes from a Coca plant, which is heavily located in multiple countries in South America, such as Columbia, Bolivia, Peru, etc. The high kicks in quickly after you sniff it, and you get extreme energy. Your whole brain will be at a rapid speed level, which your brain can't keep up with. You will spiral and become super crazy if you become addicted to it. It drives your impulse of excitement or rage at an excessive limit. You make so many poor decisions based on what you think or how you feel in the moment. If you are a person with a huge ego or with a high temper, it's going to amplify your ego and temper to an all-time high, which makes you very dangerous or just super toxic to be around. Rick James said it best, "Cocaine is a hell of a drug." So, stay off the Coke and drink some Coke. I'm talking about Coca-Cola. Pop the lid, "It's Right There!"

Crack Cocaine

Crack is a sub-creation of Cocaine, which is why it's called "Crack Cocaine." It's cheaper than Cocaine, but more addictive. Crack has made numerous drug dealers' money, and was very popular from the 80s to early 90s. It damaged the poor communities, especially the Black communities, significantly. Crack messed up everyone physically, mentally, emotionally, and soulfully in every way. It destroyed people internally and externally, for sure. It got to a point where users only wanted Crack, nothing else. There were even "Crack Houses," which were usually abandoned buildings where many users did Crack. The term "Crackhead" was invented to identify the ones who actively use it. These people spent all their money on it and even started stealing others' money, including their family members' money, to buy some more Crack. Many families were torn apart because of this drug. Some family members had to cut off a member who was actively using this because of the effects of this drug.

If someone couldn't steal money, they would have sex or give oral sex to someone in exchange for money to buy Crack or to get Crack itself. Crack became a human and life eater, with many becoming homeless from it. Plenty has gone in and out of rehab, struggling to stay sober from this drug. The ones who couldn't stay sober eventually died. On a positive note, Crack, over the next few decades, decreased in usage among the population, but it's still something to watch out for because some still use it. Don't smoke Crack! Crack the code to figure out how you can grow. The cheat code is installed inside your brain somewhere. Unlock it underneath that amazing cerebral cortex. There it is, "It's Right There!"

Heroin

Heroin is another powerful drug to damage a person. Heroin was made from Morphine and considered an Opioid, just like the pain pills I've mentioned before, along with Fentanyl. It's been around for a long time, longer than some may even think. It's not a drug that you smoke, sniff, or just take. Heroin is a drug where you use needles to inject inside your body, flowing straight into your bloodstream. It gives you an instant high, just like Crack and Cocaine. Most people who inject Heroin usually dose off sitting down or laying down, almost as it completely takes you away from reality into another world to live in, as you're not conscious of the real world. It's so potent, potent enough to kill you or give you serious medical conditions if you're using it. Plenty of people who used Heroin received different types of Hepatitis, HIV/AIDS, and more due to the overuse of needles because many users shared needles with others.

Throughout the many decades, Heroin has caused a lot of overdoses. There's a high chance that you'll never wake back up if you overuse it, whether it's your first time or even if you inject yourself daily, etc. CDC reported the Heroin overdose rate was seven times higher in 2020 than in 1999, with a 20% death rate out of all Opioids. It's currently 2023, as I'm typing this part in the book, so that's not far from 2020. That's 3, and all you need is 3; "It's Right There!" Stay away from this anti-depressant. Don't let your urge to get high and be so far away from reality let you shoot up / inject this drug inside you. The only Heroin you need is the real "heroine," which is a female hero. Everyone needs a hero and Mother Nature or a positive female figure in your life could be it. Live in reality, and if you're, in fact, a female, then become your own heroine. Hold on! It's something behind you. It's your superhero cape! Can you see it? How can you not see it? "It's Right There!"

Methamphetamine

"All my friends are Methheads." Oh! "My bad!" I messed up that song reference. I meant Metalheads from that Less Than Jake song, wrong lyric. Oops! Sorry! Excuse me for my dark humor, people. Parental Advisory is activated now for the rest of this book, even for the grown folks who still need parenting. I'm done joking. Now, let's get back to our daily programming.

Methamphetamine, also known as "Meth," is a stimulant drug. Crystal Meth, which is very potent itself, is the most used type of meth that has wrecked many lives. Usually, these users smoke Crystal Meth because the high lasts longer and is proven to be more effective compared to normal Meth. It's very addictive! You can smoke it, sniff it, inject it, or simply just take it. There are many ways to access the high of Meth in general. The chemicals inside Meth, especially in Crystal Meth, are very toxic. It's one of the most toxic drugs there is. Using this drug can also put you at risk of catching all types of Hepatitis and HIV/AIDS. Crystal Meth tears families apart also. It's very similar to Crack in its effects on people in many ways. Crystal Meth can make people very crazy by increasing their heart rates rapidly, causing many hallucinations, extreme paranoia, etc. The drug can damage your brain at a significant rate, including damaging all parts of your mouth. It's a full-body eater, and it will eat these people who care for anyone or anything that matters.

The short-term and long-term effects can both be catastrophic. Meth itself affected mostly the White community throughout the mid-west, south, and even some in the western region of America. If you're familiar with the show, "Breaking Bad," then you know all about Crystal Meth and its target consumers. Meth labs have been found all over the country, and there are some now today that are hidden somewhere. These dealers and their associates cook them anywhere, especially in places that are not around people. If you're a dealer dealing this and you get caught, you better call Saul! I gave another Breaking Bad reference. If you haven't watched that show, I highly recommend it. The show is entertaining and educational; a well-written series it is. Do not take this drug at all! Stay off the Meth and watch the New York Mets. The game is on right now! Turn on the TV! Grab the remote! "It's Right There!"

Lysergic Acid Diethylamide (LSD)

LSD, which is "Lysergic Acid Diethylamide," is a powerful psychedelic drug that is known as just "Acid" to users today. It was mainly popular from the late 60s to 70s. This drug was heavily involved in the Hippie movement, which was all about spreading love and peace around the country in vans and buses. The Hippies were all about Mother Nature, music, love, and peace. The sunshine and rainbow Symbolism came from them, as it was originally a part of their movement. LSD was considered the "happy drug." Many people who used this drug back then were listening to The Beatles, Grateful Dead, etc. The Hippies were the nicest people you'll ever meet, and they took LSD. They'll be so happy while on it, which was the reason why it was called "the happy drug."

LSD usually comes in tablet form, which is taken by inserting the tablet inside your mouth; orally used, of course. It was very easy to consume and took over America during its peak. It possesses many hallucinogenic properties, which ultimately lead to people being negatively affected by it over time. Yes, people started being happy going on psychedelic Spiritual trips, but many started hallucinating. The hallucinations can become more active and would be so intense to where people would lose their minds. With these hallucinations, many have killed themselves or even others. Plenty of users had nightmare terrors from this drug, besides hallucinating while awake. These nightmare terrors were very intense, and they haunted some forever. Short-term and long-term damage happened to people's brains. Those who received the short-term damages were able to recover, but those who received the long-term damages could never fully recover. You may have the urge to always want to be happy, but you don't need LSD for it. Instead of taking LSD, just listen to the beat, your heartbeat. It sounds nice, right? Being able to have a heartbeat and living the life is always nice. You know it! You can always be happy and make others happy if you have a heart, which is why there's a saying called "have a heart." Touch your heart and reach out to another. That person's heart is right beside you. Reach out, "It's Right There."

Psilocybin

Psilocybin, also known as "Magic Mushrooms," or simply just called Shrooms, is a psychedelic drug that usually grows in the wild. These mushrooms are natural drugs that many Spiritual people like to take. Usually, people who take this drug listen to Indie music, EDM, or other soulful music. Shrooms can take you on a journey and allow you to tap into realities that are far away from here. It can also help you reach a higher consciousness, a very deep mental state. You can discover so much about yourself, life, and the Multiverse itself with the right focus being on it. You can detect and access higher vibrational frequencies without music while on Shrooms. It's always a drug people like to experiment with, but if you're not strong enough mentally or overuse it, then it can harm you in the real world and in your dreams. You could be in big trouble if you're not careful. Stay away! Watch Out! "It's Right There!"

Marijuana

How many of you know about Mary Jane? No, I'm not talking about Peter Parker/ Spiderman's girlfriend. I'm talking about what Rick James referred to in one of his songs. I'm talking about Marijuana, also known as "Weed." Weed is a very natural drug, meaning it comes straight from the Earth/Mother

69

Nature herself. It's green just like the earth; a plant and considered a useful herb. Marijuana is more helpful than harmful compared to any legal/or illegal drug on this planet. It can be used to treat many medical conditions whether light or heavy, including curing diseases some studies have proven. Weed can also enhance your mind to a higher consciousness, allowing you to be more focused or tap in Spiritually to guide you on connecting to many things, including helping you figure things out. You can discover so much while being high on Weed if you truly concentrate on expanding your mind. Many in Ancient China would meditate to reach that ultimate enlightenment after having it. It has many pros, and I'm not talking about feeling better to relieve stress like many would say to highlight it. The pros to cons ratio is more significantly positive compared to other substances. The fact that it's more helpful to people but was illegal for many years in America, including other countries, is absurd. That's only if we're being logical.

Despite the words you just received about Weed, I do not promote any smoking of Marijuana or any other drug or tobacco products. If a substance is banned where you are located, you should never consume that substance. You are solely responsible for anything that happens to you while taking a substance like Marijuana if it's illegal in your state. Follow the laws within your jurisdiction. Your local Police Department, Sheriff's Office, the FBI, and the DEA have every right to deal with you in any way they see fit if failed to do so. That's all I needed to say on this matter. I hope you can continue to being fully informed. Thank you for receiving this message. Now, let's get back to our daily programming.

CBD and many THC products that are distributed from a factory were able to be sold legally through Vape shops in the South. They were able to find a loophole to getting high. I was surprised that it was legally sold when I first went to a Vape shop with those products. It's maybe not 100% of the real thing, but it's still a thing. CBD usually has strands of the real thing, or it's synthetic. THC, on the other hand, has strands from the real thing and is more effective than CBD. Marijuana is now legal on the West Coast and in the Northeast of America, but still illegal in the South, with some states in the Midwest included. Honestly, that's due to years of business with tobacco companies and politics more than anything. That's all I will say on the legal matter. Big companies could honestly make a lot of money off it in the South rapidly if it's ever legal. The demand would be crazy. Money, money, money!

In America, it's all about that dollar in the survival of the fittest. I've said this before, I'm just saying, "It's Right There!"

Alcohol has a more detrimental impact on mental and emotional well-being compared to Marijuana, yet the latter has often been unfairly labeled as the "bad guy." It's ironic that in today's culture, people tend to appreciate anti-heroes, and Marijuana, despite being natural with potential medical benefits and cognitive enhancements, is often stigmatized.

While Marijuana has its positives, it is sometimes overused and overly relied upon. Some people, in fact, should stop smoking it or never should have smoked it in the first place. The cons are that for most people, it can negatively affect their mental state at times, lower their senses, can make people lazy, can be just a coping mechanism for some, and can increase people's appetite, eventually making some overweight. The problem with weed is that it's more focused on as a profitable and recreational drug. Many are just addicted to the high so they can feel better and be away from reality, just like the people who use other drugs. The same code for making money off people's addiction also applies to drug dealers for weed. Weed shouldn't be used in a professional setting, nor should anyone have a weed scent on them in the workplace. If you are under the influence and make a big mistake, that's on you.

Weed can influence your sense of transparent judgment in the workplace and other life situations. If you don't need it for medical reasons, then you shouldn't always need It. Some people would smoke all day and every day without doing much in life. That's an example of people who should stop doing it or never should have in the first place. Once again, like the famous Stephen A. Smith says, "Stay off the Weed! Just cuz you high, goodbye!" Slam the door!

Now, if you're a rapper with a lot of money and you can still be professional, making a living with a respected mindset like Snoop Dogg, that's fine. The thing is, not everyone is Snoop Dogg, and a few others who I can mention. Although there are pretty intelligent and kind, active Weed smokers throughout the world, they're rare compared to the majority. It's all about the majority when it comes to influences! Weed should be taken more in edible form if you're going to use it through food or a drink. Smoking itself can still be harmful to you regardless in ways like drying the mouth, damaging your throat, etc.

Taking edibles is healthier and more natural than smoking. The only con to that is that the high takes longer to kick in, and the high rate is much higher than some can take. A few can take an edible and lose their mind going on a psychedelic trip. It may be too much for certain individuals, but it can be amazing for some to enjoy and really tap into that higher consciousness. So, if you're healthy, Weed is not what you need. You never need a substance to get through life. Wanting and needing will always be different. Get to a point where you'll be fine without it. That's all I'm saying. A sober life from drugs isn't so lame once you try it. Try it. Let me give you a new term for the word WEED. "We Evolve Every Day." That is something you need to say every day because your evolution matters. Now, try that new WEED. I just gave it to you! "It's Right There!"

Alcohol

If an individual was able to drink a whole swimming pool full of liquor, I guarantee you that people would dive into it. Kendrick Lamar was really thinking big when he mentioned the swimming pool filled with liquor in his song, "Swimming Pools." Alcohol is a legal substance that is everywhere. It's almost impossible not to be around or see it at all. Alcohol is consumed more than any drink on its own by adults from ages 21-50, other than water, of course. Alcohol is consistently advertised on billboards, social media ads, flyers, posters, commercials, TV shows, movies, and by word of mouth. It's sold in grocery stores, ABC stores, gas stations, bars, clubs, all types of venues, drink stands, and inside an alcohol brand store.

There are 3 forms of drinking alcohol. The 3 forms are beer, wine, and liquor. All 3 have different name brands, with numerous companies making their own with different colors and flavors. It can be in a can, bottle, box, or even plastic; it all depends. The market is so wide for alcohol, and it's a huge money maker. Alcohol is a very dependable money source in America. It's huge on weekends, holidays, special events, concerts, and for sporting events like the Super Bowl or the World Series. It's extremely difficult to see America without alcohol again. The first time that alcohol wasn't legal was during the Prohibition back in the 1930s. Even during the Prohibition, people were still sneaking to drink it in underground bars called "Speakeasy." It didn't last long, and eventually, alcohol was legal again. Before I get into the deep effects of alcohol that influence people, let me discuss the differences between each of the 3 forms.

Wine

Wine is considered a classy drink. Usually, wine is consumed during dinner at home, restaurants, or special events. It can also be consumed at luncheons; it just depends. It's a fine drink, as most would say. It complements some dinner meals to drink after a bite. You could try it yourself. The entrée and the wine combination is there. Chef Gordon Ramsey will even tell you, "It's Right There!" The alcohol percentages of wine can be around the single digit numbers from 4% up to the teens, like 14%. 12 to 14% are the usual alcohol percentages of wines sold inside stores. Women tend to drink wine more than men on the regular because of their preference for the taste and the way it makes them feel. Wine can make you feel very lovely in numerous ways. It's a passion drink but can also alter you if you drink too much wine. If you're a pretty damsel in distress feeling fine drinking wine, you'll need a prince charming to save you around this time. Prince Charming will catch you, but wait! You forgot your silver slipper! Look! "It's Right There!"

One very interesting thing about wine is that it can be used as a collection. Like books and art paintings, wine gets collected as a showcase/ decoration. Many bottles from different places worldwide remain unopened, dating way back to the 19th century and the early 1900s. Wine has been considered art by some well-established individuals. Wine isn't just an alcoholic drink; it's a valuable, timeless item. The Frenchman said, "Waiter, give me your finest bottle of champagne." The waiter responded back saying, "There you go, sir. The finest champagne for you. 'It's Right There!'"

Beer

Beer is the most consumed alcoholic drink in America and has been very popular in Western society for centuries. Beer has the most commercials and sponsorships and is more popular than most soft drinks. Bud Light, Budweiser, Coors Light, Michelin Ultra, Truly, and Corona are the different brands of beer you see today.

None of these companies are responsible for what you put inside your body, nor for what you do or say once you have consumed these drinks inside your body. You are solely responsible for all words and actions, including the effects on you after consumption. You must take accountability for the effects of your choice of consumption. If you never had a beer before and are cautious about drinking it, then I highly suggest that you never drink it as a sign to care about your wellbeing. It is your choice and your choice only. I, myself, am not responsible for what you decide to do. Make sure you practice safety every day and be a responsible class-act citizen. This message was brought to you by Ureh's Mind of 3. Now, back to our daily programming.

The alcohol percentage of these drinks is usually in the lower single digits to the higher single digits, like 3% to 7%. Some hit the early double-digit numbers, which an associate of mine had to remind me. He said, "You know it's some in the hood that drinks that hard beer. Come on now; 'It's Right There'"! The most popular brands of beer hit the 6% alcohol range. Beer percentages are on the bottom of alcohol level compared to wine and liquor, but it can have the same negative effects as liquor with the amount you consume. It may give you energy, make you feel better, and can bring out your personality more. It may increase the level of enjoyment for people or entertainment in general.

Although that may be true, it can also make you super emotional, like increased aggression, feeling too comfortable while making others feel uncomfortable, and slowly take away your inhibitions. The overuse of beer on a daily basis can start to alter the way you are as a person. You can slowly become an emotionally unintelligent Monster to many around you, especially the ones you love. Some men become physical and/or mental abusers of their women when addicted to beer. Over time, the buildup can affect your liver and your senses. Thousands of car accidents occurred with drivers who consumed beer before the accident. Many have died because of drunk driving. There are many deaths from drunk driving every single day. There's a higher chance of dying inside of a vehicle compared to dying on a plane. Even though there are more homicides than deaths from car accidents, you are more likely to get hit by a car than being shot by a gun, percentage-wise. Since there are many homicides in this country, I'll get a little bit off-topic to tackle that. May I?

<u>The 2nd Amendment- The Right to Bear Arms (Beer Intermission)</u>

Speaking of guns, let me talk about this real quick because it needs to be addressed. I'm sorry for going off-topic. I'll make this very quick; I promise. If you are a woman, what's the best way to protect yourself from a man who wants to harm you? A gun. If there was a zombie apocalypse right now, what's the best way to survive it? A gun. One shot to the head, dead. Guns! If America was invaded right now and the invaders came to your home right now, what's the best way for you to protect your family? A gun. That's 3, and all you need is 3; "It's Right There!" Guns! You can't fight soldiers that carry machine guns with fists and knives now. It's a reason why outsiders shy away from invading American cities, nor fight on our turf, because they know we own guns. You are safe because America is great with guns.

Men won a war killing masses to create this country with guns, they owned guns, and even hunted animals with guns. The second American right that the founding fathers thought about was having a gun. When people think about America, what do they think about? Guns! You see, I told you, "It's Right There!" Guns are a part of this country. You should know that by now. You can feel however you feel about it, but your feelings don't matter. These laws and amendments existed before your feelings existed. I'm just saying, "It's Right There!" **Now, let's get back to "It's Right There" reprogramming.** Beer on 3. 1, 2, 3, beer!

Alcohol Continued (End of Beer Intermission)

Beer

I'm not anti-beer at all. I just want everyone to be educated that if you're not responsible and/or become addicted to beer, then you can damage yourself and lose others in your life over time. You can also harm the ones you didn't know, and most of them didn't deserve the disrespect or the painful fate they received. Keep that emotional intelligence, healthy liver, and everything else that's great about you. "It's Right There."

Liquor

When T-Pain said, "Imma buy you a drink," he meant liquor, which is a hard drink. Different forms of liquor are usually brown or translucent, basically dark or light. These drinks are mostly consumed at parties, clubs, etc. It is used when people are looking forward to having a "good time" and let loose to feel better. The alcohol percentage of these drinks is usually between 14% to 45%, with a few being hard proof of percentages up to even 90%. There are different types of liquor like Rum, Whiskey, Vodka, etc. Rum is usually in the 20% range in alcohol. Whiskey is usually in the 30% range in alcohol level. Vodka is usually in the 40% range in alcohol level. There are so many name brands of each type of liquor. People are familiar with brand names like Grey Goose, Bacardi, Hennessy, Bourbon, Fireball, etc.

Once again, none of these companies are responsible for what you put in your body, nor for what you do or say once you have consumed these drinks inside your body. You are solely responsible for anything you say or do after consumption. You must take accountability for the effects of your choice of consumption. Jamie Foxx once said, "Blame it on the alcohol." You can say that, but don't blame it on the company. I'm just saying, "It's Right There!" I needed to repeat that to be very clear on this stance. Do you understand? Great! Now, back to our daily programming.

It has many varieties, and liquor can be consumed with other drinks called a "mixed drink." Some mixed drinks could be Margaritas, Mimosas, etc. People usually drink mixed drinks because of the flavor and the overall balance of everything contained in the drink. In some cases, people would drink alcohol bottles without mixing, which is called "drinking it straight." When drinking it straight, people usually take "shots." A shot is a straight drink in a tiny glass cup, single or double. Many will drink rounds of shots, getting very intoxicated by it. The more shots you take, the more of that large percentage of alcohol builds up inside your system. You might as well drink it from the bottle if you're going to order rounds of shots.

Some do drink it from the bottle, indeed. Usually, men consume liquor from the bottle the most, with most of them drinking it in the comfort of their homes due to safety reasons. Also, it's not recommended to mix dark and light alcohol together. You'll highly regret making the decision to mix both colors.

If you know, you know. You can have such a great club/party night with liquor, but you can quickly ruin the club night or party for yourself and everyone else in such a short amount of time. Liquor doesn't take much of a build-up like beer, and it can instantly take away your prohibitions and make you super emotional due to its high alcohol level in percentage. Health-wise, you're more at risk of harming yourself and others than any other drink, and that's short-term along with the long-term. It's a huge enemy to your brain cells, eyes, body movement, skin, and liver. Liquor is the main reason why there are alcohol limits with curfews enforced at public places that sell alcohol because people will drink it all night and never stop. People really lose all touch with reality with the overconsumption of liquor.

Liquor drinkers can be more violent than casual beer drinkers due to the higher percentage that they're already consuming. A liquor drinker can be the most dangerous person behind a vehicle. Henry Ruggs III is a perfect example of this. His alcohol level was excessive and way over the roof due to his overdrinking of liquor one night. He got behind the wheel that night and killed a woman who was just trying to get home. His behavior that night took an innocent life and ruined his own. His life was never the same after this incident. His image was tarnished, he lost endorsements, got released from his football team, his football career ended early, and he went to prison because of this. He was a top 5 receiver stat-wise as a young wide receiver in the NFL before this. Henry could have been one of the greatest. One night of a distraction trying to feel better with a bottle can be the worst night of your life, including other lives. It's never worth it to get behind the vehicle when you drank too much liquor, or even beer. Take an Uber, Lyft, or even have a designated driver, which is usually a friend. Drink responsibly if you're going to drink, and always think about safety. Safety is always non-negotiable. Every company, group, and person should have that policy. No one should ever get upset about safety when it comes to alcohol.

Overall, Alcohol is the most used formula for making people feel better and making life seem more enjoyable to people's standards. It's a legal formula that will continue negatively affecting the nation and worldwide. It's more common to drink socially than to never drink at all. Regardless of how you feel about alcohol, you should never say you need it. You don't need it. It needs you more than you need it, because it wants to control you or alter you. It will not get rid of your problems, nor will it make your life better. Don't let a can, a bottle, or anything else filled with alcohol feed on you. That drink will feed on your weaknesses. It will feed on all the insecurities dealing with your personality, your need to feel better due to stress or sadness, your anger, and your urge of wanting to party. You can be so amazing to talk to and be around without it. You can keep the stress and any emotion beneath the surface level without even thinking about it. You can have an amazing time at any function without even getting a sip of that drink. You're not going to blame it on the alcohol ever again because you're never going to drink it again. Break the bottle! Crush the can! That's the plan! Man! Have a glass of WATER.

Will Accelerate The Evolution Rocket. With this WATER, you'll be ready to take off at any given moment. You won't ever have to delay your flight, nor have any Technical difficulties. 100% Success rate, guaranteed. It's the finest WATER in the galaxy. You must have it! Here's a sample, try it! "It's Right There!"

Chapter 8

Spirits, Creatures, and Entities

If you made it this far in this book, then it's time to put on your thinking caps. We're about to get Biological, Astronomical, and very Spiritual. It's time to bring you deep into the horizon from here on out. Are you ready? Are you sure? It's going to be a long journey, especially to the center of the Earth. I'm sure you have time, but is your mind prepared for all that's to come? Hmm, you're already interested; I can tell. The wonder is there, "It's Right There!" Now, you're ready to receive all the information to feed your brain. Time to set out the plates and utensils to prepare for an amazing meal. This is a limited special just for you. Bon Appetit on 3. 1, 2, 3, Bon Appetit!

What do you know about Spirits, Creatures, and Entities? Some may know, but they just haven't got to the advanced part, which sometimes gets really dark. All 3 are important to have connections with. That's 3, and all you need is 3; "It's Right There!" Humans tend to mistreat Spirits and Creatures daily due to their selfish ways of not appreciating them, not trying to understand them, and due to the fear they have against them. It's a fact that Spirits, Creatures, and Entities that walk in disguise on Earth are easier to understand than humans. All 3 stick to their Multiversal code, understand the importance of their purpose, and are very consistent in a routine to serve their purpose. Humans do the opposite of that, which is why Spirits and Entities must do certain things that highly affects human just to make that all-current living things in life aren't erased. It's all about following the order of things and understanding the way of life. Natural cycles must keep flowing, or things fall apart.

Creatures

Creatures understand that they must limit themselves in a way that doesn't further affect everything connected through life. Humans don't think Creatures inherit high intelligence when, in fact, they do. They just stay in their place, respect their traditions, and do what's only asked of them; very disciplined. It might be funny to some folks to hear tradition and Creatures in the same sentence, but Creatures are very intelligent and consistent in their day to day passing all of that to their kin. It's obviously tradition, can't you see? "It's Right There." They're able to listen and adapt to the ones around them, including their environments. Cats and Dogs are entirely different, but they learn to communicate with each other and treat each other as the same inside one household, despite the difference in species. Creatures don't speak the same languages that humans can speak, but they learn to understand humans' words and body language and are able to communicate back in a way that their owners can understand. Creatures master signs, communicate, love, and overcome fear better than humans.

One thing that is very underrated is that Creatures show way more love and respect to the ones who take care of them more than a human does. Your pet can appreciate you more than your lover, kid, or parent can. I'm pretty sure all the cat and dog lovers can back me up on that. They feel that heavily and definitely know "It's Right There." You shouldn't rely on a pet to make you happy, though, because Technically, that's your job and another human's job. So please don't get too comfortable with just having you and your pets because having another human in the household is more natural. If you're a great human being – healed – then you deserve someone by your side today!

Fear of dealing with Creatures is very interesting when it comes to carnivores or even so-called "Ancient Mythical Creatures." Humans fear them very much when humans are more of a danger to them. These Creatures sense how much humans destroy each other, will kill them for pleasure, and know that humans possess weapons that can destroy life itself. Creatures understand that people are emotionally driven, want to have an unlimited supply of meat, and want to destroy their homes, messing with their daily routines. Animals have a code and live by their means. A carnivore, which is strictly meat eater, or even some bloodsuckers, are made exactly how they are. Carnivores survive off meat; it's not their fault that they were born that way. The same applies to so-called "Ancient Mythical Creatures" that appear every other year and only drink blood. It's not their fault they feed off drinking blood. It's how they survive, it's a part of their life. It's not something to fear or get rid of.

Carnivores or natural bloodsuckers aren't so-called "bad," they are on Earth for a reason. Humans fear them so much that they are trying to cage them to contain them, or eventually use them for entertainment purposes. Humans may fear them so much to mass murder them for sport to the point where these Creatures are trying to hide away from mankind, especially when it comes to Ancient Mythical Creatures. Being very afraid of what you don't understand puts that Creature in extreme danger of extinction. Many Creatures are moving up on the extinction ladder due to human behavior. Burning of trees, air pollution, water pollution, and animal overhunting are decreasing the land creatures' populations. The water pollution and overfishing are decreasing the population of Sea Creatures. Air pollution and the decrease in the population of other species are affecting Air Creatures like the California Condor, which is an endangered species according to reports in 2021. There is a cycle when it comes to every living thing on the same food chain. You all learned during Biology class in high school and just normal Science classes in the two levels of school before that. So, any decrease affects another; it's all connected, like a food web. You see, I told you, "It's Right There!" Life doesn't work properly without all these creatures from a food and lifestyle standpoint. It's possible they can all die unless humans figure out a way to thrive without them with the advancement in Technology. If the creatures die, then it's very possible humans can die too. "We're all in this together," just like that High School Musical song, team Troy Bolton.

Now, I'm not saying let's just stop eating meat completely. I'm not an anti-animal eating extremist, as I eat meat myself. I'm just saying don't abuse these Creatures, and don't abuse your hunger. A huge problem that I see when dealing with hunger, is that people eat too much meat, causing their obesity and showing more of their selfishness. Speaking of obesity, America is the most obese country in the world. It affects so many Americans, giving them long-term health problems like diabetes and heart conditions. It's proven that obesity can sometimes be passed on to the next generation. It must stop!

The biggest problem, which matters just as much as excessive meat consumption, is that many meats and other foods are being wasted daily by people. Imagine all those Creatures not even being eaten and thrown away after being killed to be eaten in the first place. You basically just wasted an animal for no reason. I'm just saying, "It's Right There!" I would hate as an animal to fight my last day against a human, knowing I'm about to be eaten, just to not be eaten at all. You would feel like your meat wasn't even delicious; that must really suck. Ultimately, the goal is not to erase creatures from planet Earth. They are a part of life, just like you are. Seriously, take the time to study these creatures. Accept them for who they are and appreciate them by giving them more of a chance to live their daily life. Don't fear any Creature that can harm you because you're a threat to them too. We can all feed on each other and still exist on planet Earth. People just got to do it right and get with the cycle of life. There's a plan to make it happen. I know you're hungry. Grab the new cookbook! Open it up! Listen carefully and please follow these instructions. You see it? How can you not see it? "It's Right There!"

Spirits

When people usually talk about Spirits they think about their ancestors, loved ones who passed away, a God, or Ghosts you see on movies and shows. Spirits could be an infinite number of possibilities, including your own soul guiding you, like I've mentioned in Chapter 1 about signs. Spirits are the extra eyes, ears, and hands. In some cases, Spirits are the doors that shouldn't be knocked on nor attempted to open, almost as if there's a "do not disturb" sign on each door. You must take Spirits very seriously and respect each Spirit. I hear a lot say Spirits are complicated when they're so easy to understand. If you block out all the noise in the world, you can hear them and feel their presence. They want you to recognize them, but out of respect and without fear. There is no such thing as "bad Spirits," but only dark and light Spirits. Dark and light are how something or someone appears and the type of energy it/they wield. It has nothing to do with intentions.

A dark Spirit could be simply serving its purpose, which could be protecting something or someone of importance. A dark Spirit could be guarding a sacred forest against any intruder regardless of any shape or form, and a human could walk through getting hurt even after the Spirit warned that certain individual to get out. In most cases, these Spirits gave them all the signs to get out or not enter in the first place, but people didn't listen. Some forbidden places still exist in this world right now, and people would die going to these places, knowing what lies ahead on their path. That's proof people test themselves, showing a lack of respect or just wanting to be harmed willingly in the first place. See, I told you, "It's Right There!"

Some Spirits that are not protecting or serving a purpose simply want to be left alone in peace. Many Spirits and even Ancient Mythical Creatures I've mentioned before ultimately want to be freed. Free to roam around anywhere they would like, free to feed on what will heal them completely or fully satisfy them, free to not be stuck in that place they've been in for centuries protecting, free to not be stuck in a place which gave them trauma, free from the place they've been imprisoned in, and free to be beyond Earth itself. How come you can't see that they only want to be free? "It's Right There!"

The term "bad Spirit" only exists because of people's fear, lack of knowledge, and/or lack of respect. There are principles of life, which include darkness. Just like in the day, you usually have a sunrise and a bright blue sky, but you have a moon and no brightness at all during the night. Light and dark make life exactly what it is. Just like there are no heroes without villains. There must be terror or no hope in order for a sign of hope like Superman to rise to the occasion, saving the day and bringing peace when there's a dark cloud over the sun. You see, I told you, "It's Right There!" In acting, there's always a part or role to play. That's what completes a story: having each type of character and the whole crew to put it all together. Doesn't that sort of remind you of a high school musical, which I've mentioned before when I said, "We're all in this together." Hmm, you see. I told you, "It's Right There!"

Entities

Before I get started on this part, if you're super Religious, then you might not believe anything that comes after this and/or feel very opinionated, which will be expected. You could feel however you feel and believe whatever you want, but sometimes you must be open and expand your mind. If you read this Chapter and conclude that I'm crazy, it honestly doesn't even matter. The only things that matter are energy and Matter itself. If you looked deeper into understanding Earth and outside of Earth, then you would know anything is possible. So much exists; it's all connected! Pay attention! The urge to ask questions and to know everything is the key. Grab the key, "It's Right There!"

Many people are not from here but have been here the whole time. Almost all of you believe that in some instances, but are not exactly sure. That's why it's a saying, "You never know who you'll meet," which is why it's important always to treat people how you want to be treated and try to understand people. Many have a hard time adapting to living among people, because humans are so complicated and fear too much, making it very hard for them to even be themselves. Some Entities are living a human experience, being in the human physical form completely with their powerful soul attached, and some are in disguise with shapeshifting abilities. You never know until you know, even if "It's Right There!" Smile for the camera if you want your memory erased, "Men in Black."

There are male and female Entities from different planets all around here. Some have arrived after the destruction of the Dinosaurs, which is Earth's first known planet reset. Some have arrived during the Ancient Egypt era, and many have arrived every now and then after. Earth is just the place to be, obviously. You know different Religions claim Earth to be a paradise. Apparently, it must be if everyone keeps coming here. I told you, "It's Right There!" Earth is the sole focus throughout the Multiverse. A planet that demonstrates life, death, and rebirth at the highest level. 3! It can always regenerate life forms, even if it must be new ones.

Speaking of female Entities, they possess more potential than male Entities. Still, many never reach their true potential because they always seem to limit themselves. When it comes to energy, there's no seniority. Anyone can be more powerful than another. The concept of men's superiority only applies to humans. Why do you think the Earth is called "Mother Nature?" Hmm, you see, I told you, "It's Right There!" Take that Religion! Yes, the shot has been fired; nothing personal. The one belief that a woman was formed out of a man's rib when every single person comes out of a woman, was in a woman's womb generally for 9 months, and for centuries was raised by a woman is completely absurd. To not even have the slightest thought of a woman being the sole creator of everything is ludicrous. You see, that's a perfect example of the human concept of men's superiority. Come on now; "It's Right There!" Use your brain, expand your mind, and leave behind all that's holding you back. That sounds like evolution, **BIG BANG!** Now, back to our daily programming.

Entities can live in paradise or have a full human experience, but many are serving a purpose; that's the angle. Just like with Spirits, there are dark and light Entities. Not every Entity is completely dark or light. There are percentages within a soul, and souls have Multiversal codes. You could wield 40% light energy and 60% dark energy, which can label you as a dark soul.

"You are what you cast," some would say. You can be a Jedi and then move to the dark side, joining The Sith, including wielding a red-light saber or dark-light saber instead of a blue or a green light saber like a Jedi would.

A lot of people are dark souls and don't even know it. Light souls are the minority in this world. In the world of power, most light elements are the beginning stages. To fully master, you must learn the dark elements. There are various dark elements that require so many skills and natural potential for greatness. Doctor Strange himself tapped into a lot of dark energy to do amazing things to defeat his enemies and keep the Multiverse afloat. He was willing to go beyond boundaries, tapping into the Darkhold and defying many laws of limitations to be in a better position to save lives while perfecting his craft of sorcery. You can't be a true Sorcerer Supreme unless you have the knowledge and the capabilities to wield dark energy successfully without it consuming you. It doesn't mean everyone should fear you if you're a dark soul, because there are many dark souls who do significantly positive deeds, just like Professor Snape in "Harry Potter." If you're unfamiliar with "Harry Potter" by J.K. Rowling, it's a fantasy world filled with magick/energy wielders, including mythical Creatures and humans. Harry Potter is the name of the main character who is the phenom of all magicians, basically, the young boy who had the potential to be the best and ended up being the best by saving the world in the end.

Harry Potter was "Slytherin" worthy and possessed many traits of a Slytherin even speaking to Snakes, but he chose "Gryffindor" instead. Gryffindor was considered a household of light magick wielders, and he had friends inside that household, along with his parents, who were Gryffindor royalty. Technically, Harry Potter has so much darkness within his code, but he chooses to mostly wield light and be in the same group as the light magick wielders. It can be said Harry Potter could be 60/40 or 50/50 himself. Professor Snape belongs to the House of Slytherin, which is considered the dark magick household within the school of "Hogwarts." Hogwarts was the most known school for all magicians, and some who went there became professors like Professor Snape. Professor Snape wielded dark magic and was the professor of the dark arts. Throughout Harry's time at Hogwarts, Professor Snape has been protecting Harry Potter many times, caring about his wellbeing at any cost. Some other dark magick wielders and Creatures also protected Harry Potter, caring about saving the world. Dark souls save lives too; even Harry Potter will tell you, "It's Right There!"

Many humans in today's world do deeds that deserve consequences where negative Karma is usually dished out. So, theoretically, Karma can be considered a dark Entity because that is what she mostly wields within her code among the humans. Yes, I'm promoting the belief that Karma is a female Entity. I know it is a Hindu concept of action regarding positive effects or consequences. Someone must be wielding that type of power, not just anybody. It's not a system. Why do you think the saying, "Karma's a bitch" exists? It's literally in the statement, as you can see. "It's Right There!"

Wielding dark magick/energy doesn't make you evil or untrustworthy. Dark souls do more to expand life, play their role, and be more disciplined than light souls. Dark souls can be loyal, respectful, and care about life too. Dark souls are so misunderstood. Although there are dark souls who can contribute to this world and the whole Multiverse for the long term, there are some who are uncontrollable and prey on the weak for personal gain, which I will mention later in this Chapter. Light souls can heal, not feed on people's weakness, etc. Light souls also can watch many people die instead of saving them, let people get hurt when they could have prevented it, and they also could do nothing to help the Multiverse expand while in any shape or form. While in human form, a lot of light souls just want to have fun living life, instead of trying to evolve people and discipline people to learn from mistakes. They're too comfortable with the privilege in this world without having a true purpose, which is not wanting to fulfill an important role that affects many others. It all depends on the soul and if they're willing to step up to the plate to be so much more.

Is Good and Bad Real?

Before I keep going on about dark and light, I want to touch up on the hero and villain scenario. "Good" and "bad" are really human terms; anyone can be "good" or "bad." It depends on the perspective/ narrative and the time frame. It doesn't generally exist when we talk about Spirits, Entities, and anything dealing with the Multiverse. 100% human concept it is. The Dark Knight, who's mainly called "Batman" from "DC Comics," usually beats up criminals and then leaves them for "Gotham PD" to lock them up. He breaks the law causing destruction to defeat people who break the law. He's considered a vigilante but the people's hero. It can be said what he does isn't so-called "good" because ultimately, instead of killing these criminals to make sure they harm no one again, he lets these criminals get the due process going to jail just for them to get released or break out, just so they can kill again. Batman knows Gotham's justice system is corrupt and that most likely these criminals will get out, so why would he put the city in more danger instead of eliminating the problem? Batman doesn't kill, though, which is a high level of humanity and ethics. But how can he be considered a real hero if his decision not to kill is a big reason more people die, including more destruction to the city? He doesn't want to kill and thinks it's not right to, but it can be proven that it's not the right decision in the long run.

Batman just shows he's unwilling to sacrifice for the greater impact and is not thinking about the long term. He is only thinking about the short term, in the moment. In a way, he's contributing. Instead of doing what needs to be done, he does what he wants to do, which isn't helping at all. Ultimately, killing a man is harder for him; beating someone up is easy. Batman fears what he will become and what would happen to him if he started killing villains, which makes his deeds more about him if you really think about it. So, in a way, Batman is not willing to give it his all and do the hard things. In conclusion to that, Batman isn't saving lives at all in the end. He's just giving villains another time to kill people and destroy the city. I know it's hard to accept that, but "It's Right There!" I love Batman, he's super smart and skilled while looking so cool as the wealthy character that he is. It's nothing personal against Batman, it's just a truthful assessment.

A lot of these so-called "heroes" think about the short term, not the long term. Are you really saving people if there's no future for them right after? That's a serious question to be asked. The true villain, often overlooked, is the end of the Multiverse—the consequence nobody anticipated. In some cases, the most potent forces or individuals operate in obscurity. True power prefers silence and invisibility. I get you couldn't see, because it wasn't right there. See, the end of the Multiverse is the real villain of the Multiverse through films and in real life. Turn on the TV, take notes. Look! "It's Right There!"

Anti-Matter Human God Theory

An Anti-Matter God could manipulate anything of Matter and energy and use humans as a vessel just like Agent Smith does in "The Matrix." I call this The Anti-Matter Human God Theory, which is a dark entity from an Anti-Matter Universe that survived the Big Bang, who's gaining control of humans with fear as its most used weapon to manipulate humans and everything human uses to create another Big Bang where Anti-Matter could be all that matters figurately speaking. The ultimate human killer, the ultimate virus, the ultimate planet destroyer, and the ultimate Universe destroyer is an Anti-Matter God. Some could say that sounds like the "Anti-Monitor" from DC Comics who absorbed energy from the Multiverse to power himself, helping the Anti-Matter Universe grow while the Multiverse declines. Within this Multiverse, along with so much undiscovered in a big Space of unlimited energy, anything is possible. Everything you do or think that doesn't matter is Anti-Matter, figuratively speaking.

When individuals fail to realize their true potential and instead bring about destruction rather than nurturing life, the Multiverse weakens. This weakening potentially empowers Anti-Matter, according to theoretical considerations. The Law of Conservation of Mass/Matter explains that when Anti-Matter and Matter come together in equal measure, they mutually annihilate, leaving behind only energy. This process essentially restructures Outer Space, initiating a new beginning.

Consider the possibility that, in the future, everything could be comprised of Anti-Matter. The Multiverse demands a substantial return, yet humanity seems to be falling short. Numerous movies and shows depict a narrative where humans, ultimately, destroy all living things. Although these plots often introduce a hero with the assurance that "humans will change," hints of the Multiverse's impending end are occasionally mentioned by anti-heroes, only to be ignored. It's not just some type of propaganda, which some said online about that narrative. It's very realistic, and you must not be in denial.

Perfected Super ASI in certain shows and movies see the threat, including current ASI, so they take necessary precautions just like the machines did in The Matrix. That's just my deeper take on how I view The Matrix from a symbolic foreshadowing of the real world, and I've heard Biblical deep takes from some others on how they view The Matrix. The Biblical take is that Neo was like Jesus, making the ultimate sacrifice to save the people, to give humans another chance. Films always focus on saving the people, highlighting the short term, which is the death of the people. Saving the people is always Hollywood priority, even if it risks the future of everything no longer existing. A lot of people fail to catch that. Silently, it's been there the whole time. "It's Right There."

These heroes' emotional attachment to humans is what makes them not even think about the end of all existing Matter at all, nor take it seriously like it doesn't matter. They're wrong! It does matter more than anything! I just told you, and you obviously see what's going on in the world right now as "It's Right There!"

This Anti-Matter God and the ones controlled by this individual will erase everything as a long-term action in the future if it's not taken seriously. There is no future along as that Anti-Matter like energy is growing stronger without being discussed to fight against it. All lifeforms no longer existing is very realistic! Do not rule out that possibility if you can't see ahead. Human selfishness, with all the influences that negatively affect them, can put more of the Anti-Matter God in the driver's seat to wreck the beautiful vehicle that we all have been riding in. Life! Everyone who watched The Matrix knows Agent Smith was another program but theoretically in reality, it's possible he could be an Anti-Matter God that disguised himself as a program and took over all the programs and humans inside The Matrix.

Machines and humans had a common enemy for a reason, which is why The Machine City let Neo go through to face him. Neo was "The One," he was a Universal prophet in each timeline. As we all know, there have been different versions of The Matrix and The One. Hmm, that sounds like different timelines to me. What do you think? I'm just saying, "It's Right There." Except in this prophecy, he was meant to defeat the Anti-Matter God, not the machines this time around. This version of Neo in the Multiverse was able to wield power in the real world. A regular human can't do that; only an Entity can, and Entities can wield massive energy, being powerful as the protectors of the Multiverse. You see, I told you, "It's Right There!" Now, to some of my hardcore Science nerds who only believe the text and nothing else without trying to further examine people and life for themselves, I already figured out what some of you may think about that. It's a reason why I said "like," "figuratively speaking," and "theoretically." I was prepared for this moment. All yes, I was! I just have one thing for you. Don't get your panties caught in a wad; it's just a theory. I'm just saying, "It's Right There!"

Uncontrollable/Controllable Souls

As mentioned earlier in this Chapter, there are uncontrollable dark souls. Some dark souls who prey on everyone for personal gain can serve something much bigger than themselves, following orders in key moments. It can be hard to believe to most that dark souls who feed on people's weaknesses, ignorance, and fear can be of service in the long run. I'm aware of this, which is why I need to explain. Believe it or not, most of these souls are living by their means, doing what they naturally do within their Multiversal code to survive while serving the role of making it difficult for the people in order for them to grow. They are there to separate the strong from the weak. People must be tested and not have it easy to reach their true potential. How can you learn if you're always getting what you want and have never been taught a lesson? That's why being a human can be a privilege despite the many cons, because you can learn the most as a human. Everyday breathing on planet Earth as a healthy human with all 5 senses is a privilege. These souls do what they do for them and for the future, which creates powerful individuals who overcome all the adversity. They're a part of everyone's journey and essential in life, regardless of how anyone feels.

Although we talked about the controllable dark souls, some dark souls are uncontrollable and can't stop. The concerning part is that the number of the uncontrollable is growing rapidly due to the world's influences. It could be said that maybe the Anti-Matter God is just a dark Entity from this Multiverse who's a hybrid, who's indifferent towards humans, and oversees the negative influencing on humans just so they can cause complete destruction to themselves, maybe so. What you think? Take 3 mins to think about that and discuss.

It's true that these uncontrollable very powerful dark energy wielders are considered the "worst of the worst," "Sabotaging Gods." Very few of these individuals are highly skilled with a massive power level but have been actively toying with the people freely. The other specific individuals of Entities were tortured so much in the human experience that they became the torturers. Their time on Earth, whether in any form, could have influenced them so negatively, even if their time was lovely. They don't care about anyone or anything and will do everything they do until their last breath. They usually say, "We're all going to die anyways." They just told you! Watch Out! "It's Right There!"

Chapter 9

Secrets of The Multiverse

Play some Space Rock listening to Angels and Airwaves while I take you on "The Adventure." If you are ready to board this spaceship to travel Outer Space, then buckle up and prepare as we take off. 1, 2, 3, lift off! If you want to figure out everything in life, the quickest way to get there is by 3 specialized subjects. The 3 specialized subjects are Ancient History, Astronomy, and Spirituality. If you master all 3, then you'll unlock every door. That's the key, grab the key, "It's Right There!" Physics is the most important one of all.

Now, the 4 main subjects in school are Math, Language Arts, History, and Science. They're the 4 main subjects for a reason, and that's to the core. Core subjects! A lot of simple-minded people would claim they aren't needed just like they say school isn't needed, when in fact the subjects themselves and school are needed. School conditions you to learn. Without knowledge, you are powerless and wouldn't know how to do anything, nor would you have a brain to use. School conditions you to wake up early, be at a place at a certain time, and stay wide awake for hours while following orders from your superior. School conditions you to do a bunch of work that you don't like to do, including some that's unnecessary. If you haven't noticed, that sounds like the everyday life of an average adult. You wake up early for a job, must be at work at a certain time, or you'll be late, and you listen to a manager and/or supervisor or anyone that's above your position. Finally, you do a bunch of work that you hate doing and think is pointless, but you have done it anyway because it's in your job description. See! I fucking told you, "It's Right There!"

Being graded in school is also a great system because it maintains a mental and physical standard. So, if you are smart and figuring things out, you'll be recognized for your intelligence and for making things easier. If you work hard, you can complete anything in life, and hard work is how you win. If you really want something, you get it. School teaches you that you will be rewarded for being smart and working hard, which is serving. You receive the basics on how to be a winner. It's a successful program if you're committed to learning. The principles of life; "It's Right There!" School!

Remember, the smartest in the world is the most powerful person in the world. The 4 main subjects are for you to master life and are required for you to be brilliant and exceptional. Those subjects are connected. Science itself is connected to everything existing with Matter and energy. There's no future without Science. I'll debate with anyone about it, there's too much proof. Spirituality is even heavily based on the Astronomy part of Science. The word "evolution" itself comes from Science. That's becoming better, or expanding, or changing from one thing to another. Science! None of these words exist without Science. Coming up with medicines and Technology was based on Science. Science is the study of everything, the application of knowledge. It's questioning and experimenting to find out the facts of every aspect of life.

Without Science, you wouldn't have any knowledge at all. You wouldn't understand anything, not even yourself or how you came about without Science. Language Arts is needed to communicate and decipher all forms of communication, like Hieroglyphics or even soundwaves of frequencies. History is data, the past and present, that you or someone just recorded/wrote down. Math is to put it all together, the equations using all the orders of operation to come up with solutions. Science is the curiosity that started the whole process and is the result of what you just discovered after you figured out the solution with Math. You see, I told you, "It's Right There." Science, Language Arts, History, Math, Science. In that order again, and again, and again. "It's Right There!"

Humans

The Bible talks about all the deadly sins and other stuff, but what people can't comprehend is that the "Bible" is subliminally saying humans themselves are a sin, a walking sin. It was an underline the whole time. Humans are capable of all the deadly sins; those are traits only they have, and those are everything in humans' true dark nature. Oh, you never comprehended that, how could you not? "It's Right There!" The whole purpose of a human on Earth is to become a God or Goddess in some way; that's the secret. You can't live in paradise if you're always suffering, having problems, and acting out of emotion. Once you're out of the loop/maze/ matrix, you realize who you truly are and what you can do when you're no longer brainwashed. The brain is the key to everything. The smartest is the most powerful once again; that's why the saying "knowledge is power" exists.

You must be like a young Lord Voldemort wanting to know everything, questioning anything that matters because he wanted to know the secret truths and figure it all out to apply. I'm not saying you should also commit all the same things as Lord Voldemort. Come on now! I was not really promoting you to be exactly like "He whose name we cannot say," which is the dark lord who's the antagonist to Harry Potter. If you think I would be foolish enough to do that, then you haven't been comprehending anything, and I highly suggest you stop reading this book. Grab the cover and close it. "It's Right There!" I'm just joking! Everyone needs a little humor here and there inside this emotionally driven society nowadays. The point is that there's only one way to no longer be a sin: don't be human anymore.

You'll have to evolve and become so much more. When you evolve and become something much bigger and can defy all laws of Physics to become an "Unstoppable Force," what is that? That sounds like a God. I'm just saying, "It's Right There!" God or Goddess, indeed, is what you can be. You see, I told you, "It's Right There!" I know some of my Religious folks are saying, "This is where I stop reading this book." I promise that I will make up for it later if you continue reading. If you don't, then that's on you. I'm not responsible for your feelings, you are!

I'm just saying and being very logical about it. That's the only way to no longer be a sin, Technically. You can control your destiny, be smart, and be powerful instead of being powerless depending on someone else having no true destiny at all. Everyone can be a superhero in their own movie. Evolution is unlimited! Your evolution can always increase and it's for anyone and anything, which is all of Matter. There are no limitations on what you can do or know. You can be as powerful as you can be, but that's all up to you. If you're worthy enough and become fearless and study everything about life, then you can. Making other people powerful is the best way to become powerful. It's beneficial to you, to the other person, and to the Multiverse. It's the long-term contribution that can be infinite.

Energy is unlimited! So, you can absorb all the energy inside this Multiverse to become an "Unstoppable Force." Capabilities are unlimited! Most humans were made from stars! You're a fucking star! Shine! Entities don't just do whatever, either. As I said, they serve a higher purpose: being powerful to power the Multiverse to keep the Multiverse afloat while possibly expanding it. Your evolution helps out the Multiverse! It expands life, and you'll be able to create infinite lives. It shall be grand, but with a slam. Grand slam! No fear should let you shy away from this responsibility because it's extraordinary. All Matter and energy is the creation of all of us. **BIG BANG!** In the Cosmos, the only thing that can stop you is you. Look in the mirror! It's there! "It's Right There!"

The Multiverse

If you have read this book and made it this far, you'll know I've been saying "the Multiverse" very often. The Multiverse does exist along with the infinite timelines of the Universe. Many have another version of them in another timeline. Your soul can't be 100% the same in another timeline if it's another you, but it can be very similar in ways. The "Mandela Effect" is a Multiversal effect, according to my deep observation mixed with my prior knowledge before this world programmed me. Some will notice certain changes in a current timeline, some won't. The ones who noticed the most changes and/or every change are able to crossover, along with having fewer versions of them across the timelines. You could have sworn someone died many years ago and then suddenly just recently died in your timeline. You were right! You saw the change. "It's Right There!"

Time is very tricky sometimes, especially inside the Multiverse with alterations being made here and there also. Real-time can seem like forever or can go by quickly. Time can shift in numerous ways when dealing with Multiversal travel or Multiversal issues. If you're able to connect to a dimension where time isn't much of a factor, then you can do big things that can affect real time and/or the future. Multiple realms exist outside of real-time, and the "Spirit Realm" is one of them. The Spirit Realm can be accessed if you're able to astral project at a high-frequency rate to enter the many dimensions. When you're busy in these other places, you sometimes lose real-time; it can go by quickly.

I've mentioned in Chapter 1 that time is everything and can't be defeated, but it's possible to reach certain agreements with it or manipulate it. That statement in Chapter 1 applies mostly to beginners because most beginners waste their time and don't respect time. You could use time to your advantage, which is why I say do what matters and figure out everything. You're going to want time on your side. What if it's possible to control time itself, but not just in one Universe, the whole Multiverse. I'll get back to you on that later in life. There might be a certain someone who will attempt to do that, and maybe will be successful on doing so. I'm just saying, watch out! "It's Right There!"

A common term used in the Multiverse is "Déjà Vu." This term is used when people experience things that they feel like they've experienced before. What people don't realize is that you did experience it before. You did it, but in another timeline, or doing it again in the current timeline. Sometimes, you can have memories you created in another timeline when you crossover, memories the other you created within that timeline, and time itself can also manipulate and control you. That is why I've mentioned being stuck in the loop and how much of a big boss time is. Time can fight with you too, that's why you should understand it and try to be on the same side at least. There's no exact calculation of how much energy and mass there is outside of Space. You can't get an exact number on infinity.

Although I love Quantum Physics, there have been some studies that rule out the idea of a Multiverse like it doesn't exist. "Boo! That sucks," the audience said. I know; I totally understand where they're coming from. The best thing about Science is that there's always new Science that beats out the old Science. Am I right? It's all about proving or maybe getting more advanced/more updated with time. The Quantum Physics realm boasts some of the brightest minds in Science, but not everyone in the field shares the same brilliance. What! I'm just saying, "It's Right There." I genuinely admire the work of the ones I'm talking about, yet that doesn't exempt them from a grand natured roast… If you know, you know.

Some physicists cling to the belief in a singular Universe simply because that's what they've been taught. Their struggle lies in an inability to fathom the broader certainty of existence beyond their limited perspective. Their panties were caught in a wad, we were too late. They deny what has already been expanded before their existence, which was the multiplication of the Universe. Remember when I told you, "These laws and amendments existed before your feelings existed?" You see, Kang The Conqueror would even tell you, "It's Right There!"

The Importance of Religion

Religion has been very influential in the world for centuries. It gave masses over the centuries a purpose in life, including how to live daily. You must have a purpose! Even though I'm not Religious, I can honestly say there are many adults from ages 18 to early 30's who need Religion. It can also be said that Religious adults around that age need to commit more to their faith. That's why the term "practice what you preach" exists. You must walk the walk, if you talk. How could you accept anyone believing in your cause if you're not fully invested? It's crucial to fully commit to something you soulfully believe in. That's the key, grab the key, "It's Right There!"

Religion can save some from doing internal and external damage. There are many Religions like Christianity, Judaism, Islam, Hinduism, etc. There are different practices of some of those Religions like Christianity have Protestants, Catholics, and Jehovah's Witnesses. Some of these Religious members disagree with each other on the differences in their practices. Even though Religion can prohibit you from expanding your mind and dampen some of your abilities to fully evolve, you can learn so much from Religion and be able to use it to your advantage. Religion teaches so much that you can absorb and be accustomed to everyday. In this world today, I understand Religious people more than people who aren't Religious or Spiritual, which is like half of the Liberal population, honestly.

Please don't get offended as I mentioned in the intro and in numerous parts of this book. If you're super offended by my recent statement, then you can stop reading this book at any given time if you would like. I am not in control of your feelings nor your time, you are. One thing I can do is make a promise to inform you of all I know, and all the info that's contained in this book will help you. Remember about the listening to the WORD line in Chapter 3, which I refer to as, "Will Overcome Real Disadvantages." The WORD is to uplift people, start their day, and is spoken when the odds are stacked against them. So, when you listen to the WORD, you Will Overcome Real Disadvantages. You're going to be uplifted, you will have a great day, and you will defeat all the odds that

are stacked against you. In church, you hear the **WORD** all the time to be uplifted to start your day, which is on the first day of the week. **Sunday! See; "It's Right There!" Listen! Let's continue if you are willing to control your emotions and hear the rest. Shall we continue? On the count of 3. 1, 2, 3, Religion!**

Religion teaches people discipline, patience, unconditional love, principles, morals, tradition, values, sacrifice, and structure, such as the importance of having a full family household and order in the world. The United States of America was built off these same foundations, but through the Protestant way. Religion teaches us that sometimes humans need limitations, that they must get rid of their pain, not be too selfish, and that there are consequences for certain actions. Respecting time is key within Religion. Many Christians always say, "Your time will come, believe it!" Self-control has always been something Religions have expressed repeatedly to people. Loving people no matter what, accepting them for who they are, and practicing forgiveness is essential in so many ways.

You must believe in people too, that they will find their way on the right path at some point. A man and a woman must have certain principles they go by because having something you abide by helps you take accountability and responsibility. Principles can help with your morality, and having great morals means showing respect for yourself, including your soul. Great morals prepare you to be a lifelong partner with someone and worthy to be trusted to have a bond or partnership with. Tradition allows you to be very consistent in what you have and do. Consistency is key to dependency and the key to building a family legacy. You can't pass down something grand and valuable from generation to generation, nor build a powerhouse without tradition. Speaking of values, values matter. Commitment, Communication, Emotional Intelligence, Compassion, Empathy, Gratitude, Honesty, Humility, Kindness, Loyalty, Openness, Passion, Reliability, Respect, and Vulnerability. These are some important values which these Religions teach. All these values are great to have, and nobody can deny that.

Marriage is the biggest commitment Religions promote between two people, and a lot shy away from that today based on fear. The sex before marriage thing is more common among people after my studies on the lustful, broken people of today, but the sex after marriage thing is more beneficial towards a union between two people. Believe it! Fun Fact: The Multiverse loves arranged marriages. Obviously, that could never work today for most of you; I just wanted to mention that. You could forget I even said that. Marriage is important, though. It's not just committing to spend your life with someone else and committing to create life with someone else, but it's also a huge service to the Multiverse, which I've mentioned before. When you get married, you are making the Multiverse happy, showing appreciation for existing, and basically telling the Multiverse that you want to expand life itself. Getting married and creating a baby collectively is one of the greatest things a human can do.

Sacrificing is the most unselfish thing a human can do. It defines how much a person is willing to give up in order to serve and/or get what they deserve in time. Sacrifice is essential in life regardless. It's part of moving forward/ letting go to receive so many great things. You may lose something/ someone special when you sacrifice, but the reward is so much greater. It is grand, but with a slam. Grand slam! Life never leaves you hanging for your sacrifice, it will appreciate you and return the favor by a large margin. There was a loss, but eventually, there came a win, and that win can be life-changing. Having structure is the foundation/ the walls that keep everything together, so even a family legacy can't make it long-term if it isn't a full household. Without that family structure, it will fall apart and never have dominance or decline in dominance. Without order, there's chaos, and things will never make sense with the possibility of no progression at all.

The biggest thing that's so amazing about Religion, which I find very fascinating, is that it teaches people to serve something much bigger than themselves! Religion does that better than anything else in the entire world. Now that I can agree with any Christian, Muslim, Jew, etc. It teaches people not to be influenced by the world, to separate from it in the many practices inside these Religions. You don't have to believe it, but you can listen to the WORD and learn real stuff that you can apply to your everyday life. You can learn from anything, anyone, everything, and everyone. Many of these Religions have some truth in them, with similarities and common ground with one another. See, it's a bit of everything. Everything is connected like I've mentioned before. Never just close your ears when someone of another Religion, or someone of a Religion is speaking their material. Let them speak! You can learn something new from even one thing they say, or you can hear

100

something you needed to hear right in the moment. Once you hear that one thing; it will click. It will resonate inside you, and you'll feel it inside your soul too. Now it's' implanted in your brain forever. I don't have to tell you. You'll know, "It's Right There!"

Ancient Cultures

Studying Ancient Cultures can be such an eye opener to anyone who digs deep into it, especially the ones who question things early on in life. Learning about the different Ancient Cultures teaches so much about this Earth and is the foundation of life, which powerful people from America even stood by when creating this powerhouse of a country. They give you more of an insight into how things started before the heavy influence of Religions, which is basically getting to the bottom of the truth.

Ancient Cultures date way back before the first human cleansing, which is the second Earth cleansing of all living things. The first cleansing of all living things was when meteorites crashed into Earth while Dinosaurs roamed the land. I will not dive deep into Dinosaurs, but I'll talk about powerful Reptile Creatures here very soon. Ancient Egypt, Ancient Rome, Ancient Greece are the 3 main Ancient Cultures. Their symbols, ways of life, and things they've created are still used today in some places. These cultural beliefs became a myth to the world of today when these cultures invented so much, including things connected to everything. They were ahead of their time and created many sources of power, which a small group of powerful individuals wield today. How could it be a myth if their practices are being used in a way that affects humans? The many rituals and lessons taught can be beneficial to humans forever.

Ancient Rome

Ancient Rome gave us Architecture, Roads, Social Institutions, Politics, Gladiators, and Medical Tools for warriors in war. Julius Caesar is the reason why we have a 12-month calendar; we had 9 originally. That's a fun fact. The real new year starts in March; welcome my non-History reading folks. They had many Gods and rulers in their History. The Roman Gods had the same names as the planets in our Solar System, very symbolic indeed.

Ancient Greece

Ancient Greece gave us Architecture, Sports including the Olympic Games, Drama/Theater, Math like Geometry, and Western Philosophy like Democracy or Theocracy, etc. It was proposed that the Ancient Greeks believed in the Big Bang sort of. "It's a warm summer evening in Ancient Greece." If you're into the Big Bang Theory while teaching Physics, Dr. Sheldon Lee Cooper will even tell you, "It's Right There!"

When you think of Ancient Greece, you think of Zeus, Athena, Poseidon, and Ares. These Gods and Goddesses were legendary, as were their creatures. Speaking of their Creatures, most Creatures that Christians claimed to be "Demons"/evil, in fact, are Ancient Greek Creatures. A "Satyr" and many others were not considered vile Creatures according to Greek Culture, nor under the orders of Satan because that name was never mentioned as it didn't exist at the time. These Creatures and the Ancient Greek Culture, in general, existed before these Religions existed. If you look closely at the timeline in History with Greek Culture and the other Ancient Cultures, it proves it to be so.

Even when talking about timelines in History, many names of humans existed before "Adam and Eve" were ever introduced. Ancient Egypt's distinct human names are a perfect example of my point, before the Babylon era. It was claimed by a few sources that some Babylonians told the story of Adam and Eve. More common names like Adam and Eve didn't exist in the early centuries of human existence, nor did they become a norm until many centuries later, even centuries past Western Society takeover. The names from Ancient Greece, Ancient Egypt, Ancient Rome, and Babylon are very different from Adam and Eve. There's no way you start off with those simple human names, then come with symbolic fancy names, then many centuries later decide to do simple names again, which are very European based. Common sense is your best friend, and History is data. You can't argue with data and common sense combined. Look! "It's Right There!"

Speaking of the timeline once again, I noticed seeing "Athena's," the Goddess of Wisdom, name multiple times throughout the timeline. A normal person can't live that long to appear multiple times with many years apart. I saw it! Before the Mandela Effect, it was there! "It's Right There," I said. The term "Atheist" comes from opposing the Greek Gods originally. Ancient Greeks said that Zeus constantly interfered with humans' lives, causing distrust among the people, so people stopped believing in him. The term Atheist comes from "Atheos," which is without the Gods or as easy as saying Godless. I like to say the "Athe" part in Atheist is like "Athens," which is a landmark city in Greece. That tells you where it comes from. So Technically, the word Atheist wouldn't even exist if it wasn't for the Greek Gods existence. That's very interesting for a so-called "myth." See, I told you, "It's Right There!"

Ancient Egypt

Ancient Egypt, which was originally known as "Kemet," gave us cosmetics, calendar and timekeeping, and hieroglyphs/Symbolism. Ancient Egypt had many Gods and rulers called "Pharaohs" in their History. These Gods and Pharaohs were considered to be superior to other Ancient Cultures. Now, let's dig very deep into Ancient Egypt. Ancient Egypt is the source of many past, present, and future things. 3! So many theories circulated around the advanced structure of Kemet, the symbolic languages presented, and the intelligence from there in general. It's the most fascinating time in History for Historians. There are so many undiscovered truths about Ancient Egypt/Kemet still to this day.

The most talked about subject dealing with Ancient Egypt, is the structure of the pyramids. Pyramids represent strength, aspiration, or a reminder of a ruler. It was way ahead of its time, too perfect. The structure was said to be too mathematically aligned for any human to figure out. It's one of the world's wonders. Pyramids in Egypt and other places built in Ancient Times of any culture are a source of massive energy. The pyramids absorb so much energy, but exactly for what? Many still can't figure it out, but I'll tell you. The pyramids are like keys, keys that stay inside the gateways throughout this Earth. Once it draws enough energy, the keys turn to open up portals. One day, these portals will open, and the rest will be History. That's the key, grab the key, "It's Right There!"

Ancient Egypt absolutely displays intelligence that's not from Earth. In Chapter 8, I've mentioned that the different Entities that people of today would call Aliens, have been around for a long time since Ancient Egypt. They've landed and made their mark with all their plans intact, still in progress. There's so much that people don't know or are too scared to know. The hieroglyphs themselves show many non-humans walking on this Earth. These hieroglyphics tell stories of History whether from past, present, or the future. Speaking of time, it can be said that the Ancient Egyptians had a deep connection with time. An hourglass was very significant in their culture and in History generally. The hourglass is super symbolic, bringing up mysteries about Space and time dealing with these Ancient Egyptians.

A few of those hieroglyphics I was talking about are deep messages to unlock certain things if you speak the correct tongue. You may need to slither with your tongue. SSS!!! There was so much power within that era, and the practices within that culture that were very significant on a large scale. As I've mentioned, ancient Egypt also had many Gods and Goddesses. The most famous one is "Heru," who's commonly known as "Horus." Horus is the Greek translation of Heru. Heru/Horus's symbol of his one eye has been a symbol that held power for many years and still holds power even now. The Eye of Horus is very significant and is very positive. It's a reminder of Horus, but it represents health, restoration, and protection. The Eye of Horus, the pyramids, and more are on the American dollar for a reason.

A lot of brainwashed folks of today see the Eye of Horus or anything Ancient Egypt-related and think it's evil when it's not. It's special! Ankh, also known as the "Key of Life" symbol, represents life itself. The Key of Life being worn as a necklace is quite interesting, and that's only because "The Cross" looks exactly like it and is worn the same way. If you look closely at the timeline in History, you see what came before. I'm not getting into all the details. I'm just saying, "It's Right There!" If the Key of Life had never existed, who knows if that other symbol would have appeared. An eye emoji, like the Eye of Horus would have been perfect to insert right after that line. If this was a picture book, I would have put it right there!

The Snake has always been a huge symbolic Creature, more than Scorpions to Ancient Egyptians, like a "Cobra." Reptiles have always been a big factor in Ancient Egypt. If you dig deeper into the Entities that landed and/or been on

Earth during Ancient Egypt, you'll find out that there are many Reptile-like forces of different types that have been ruling since the beginning. A few Pro-Ancient Kemetic people will even discreetly tell you that their ancestors were walking Reptile Goddesses. You thought I had forgotten about that, didn't you? I told you I would touch base on that to make the proper connection. I just had to make sure I spoke the correct tongue. Excuse me if you heard a little slither with my tongue. SSS!!! "It's Right There!"

Secret Societies

Before I discuss the purpose of Secret Societies and everything about it, giving another perspective for people to understand it without fear and misconception, one thing must be understood. I highly respect every Religious person who's living up to what they preach about, having their standards, and keeping their tradition or way of life alive. I can honestly say that the Jews have done an outstanding job on this planet with how they think, how they carry themselves on the daily, and the major contributions they've contributed to the world for many centuries. It was grand, but with a slam. Grand slam!

A reason why Judaism is the oldest Religion known to mankind is because you can't outdo the originators. Originators will always find a way to keep creating, to keep rising, setting the tone. The commitment to any faith or monumental belief defines a person's strength of obedience and strength of trust, which is trusting that they will be rewarded for their service with the idea that there is an ultimate plan for all living things. No matter what you or anyone believes in or disagrees on, we all want the world to be a better place forever. If you're evolving every day, giving the WORD, listening to the WORD, doing what matters, serving something much bigger than yourself, carrying yourself with class, then you have everything to be proud of. Whether you're a Religious person, Spiritual, or even a Scientific person; we could all play a role in reshaping the world.

That's where Secret Societies come in: individuals with different beliefs coming together and having common goals to serve one purpose. The purpose is to keep the world properly functioning, doing what's best for the long term.

Secret Societies serve the Multiverse and are groups that have been trusted to have the responsibility to make all the very important hard decisions in this world. Secret Societies plan small and big events, making huge sacrifices for what's best at the time, or for the future. These decisions require a lot of discipline with almost no emotion for various reasons. Some of these decisions may be what's best for them internally also, but it does put them in a better position to keep on serving.

These people are the 1%, the most important people in the entire world. They've committed their physical form and soul to serve the realm. Protectors of Earth Realm! Mortal Kombat! Scientists, inventors, businessmen, celebrities, politicians, and other government officials are part of Secret Societies. Brothers, sisters, cousins, parents, etc. A lot of power and wealth is within these groups. America was structured by Secret Societies. The founders of America were members and passed on the tradition to their families from generation to generation. Most who are in power or of high profile are a part of that brotherhood. There are multiple Secret Societies, which some may already know. There's no need for me to list the names at this point. If you know, you know. What you need to know is that Secret Societies are important and have been misunderstood. Without Secret Societies, it's believed humanity and all current life in this world would have died already or that the world wouldn't have advanced this much. They keep the world in order or keep order in the world, which is very crucial.

These members created laws and amendments for the people to abide by, and they were created for many reasons, including for the people's own benefit. These laws and amendments existed before your feelings existed. This is a saying everyone should remember by now, especially the laws and amendments today, which people get so upset about when America was built on these laws and amendments. It's all a part of America. You could feel however you feel, but it's documented in everything, including many books. Look! "It's Right There!" There was a lot of thought made into each law with so much logic and extreme strategic measures for the grand benefit of the long term. Members also have laws and a way of life that exceeds everything else they created for the people. Secret Societies abide by the "Old World," which is living by Ancient Principles, Ancient Laws, and conducting Ancient Practices. 3! All the Ancient Ways from Ancient Egypt, Ancient Rome, and Ancient Greece, but mostly connected with Ancient Greek customs. These individuals are, in fact, traditional and tap into every source of power there is on Earth. For example, you could find the Ancient Symbolism anywhere on even American money, art in museums, and throughout important buildings like the White House or at a Lodge.

These highly respected individuals know all the secrets to Earth and this Multiverse. Yes, they get powerful, wielding all types of energy, but they serve a higher purpose that is more important than anything. They've been playing their role amazingly, which is why they get what they deserve. I've said earlier that the goal on Earth is to become truly free, evolving, becoming as powerful as you can be while contributing to the natural order of things in life to best serve the Multiverse. Scroll back up. See, I told you, "It's Right There!" People always complain about how much power even one individual has, forgetting one important thing. With power comes plenty of responsibilities. So how can a certain individual hate if they are too full of fear to even step up to the plate and take on numerous responsibilities? That sounds like a personal problem to me; jealousy, envy, and deflecting off themselves. Hmm, my "Spidey Senses" are tingling. I sense haters. The haters, look, they're right there! If you're rich, being on your best behavior, and sticking to entertaining, that's when they will only love you.

Masses of today have so much hate for successful people who don't entertain them. They hate that they weren't ambitious, disciplined, or smart enough to figure out life to get where these members are; they are extremely frustrated with their failure. Believe it or not, people also hate that they don't understand your mission. So, if you're doing big things to reshape the world and they can't understand the things you're doing or can't understand you at all, then they're going to hate on you at some point; It's inevitable. Accept it, "It's Right There!" If you're a new Secret Society member or new to the wealthy club, be prepared. Watch out! "It's Right There!"

Before I spoil the Fate of the World, let me inform you about Fraternities and Sororities compared to Secret Societies. The usual Fraternities and Sororities are basically replicas of Secret Societies. I know some will get so upset about what I said if they're in one, or if you're in one of those, but it's true. Facts defeat feelings on any given day. "Sorry; I aint sorry." (Beyonce)

Secret Societies are the real thing dealing with real Ancient Greek Traditions, while Fraternities and Sororities are copycats. HBCU's have Fraternities and

Sororities that they're in control of, which backs up my statement because Greek stuff is not even a part of Black people's culture at any time in History. But they still present Greek symbols as if it's their way of life. I know that stings hard. Ouch! The bumblebee had to die by now. I'm just saying, "It's Right There!" They're Secret Society-ish, which is like but not exactly. They're the great value version as some folks would say, sorry Walmart. They're not a part of the order, 322. They're not free, builders. They have some similarities, but Secret Societies are on a higher pay scale and a higher effective rate with way more responsibilities, which is more power, as I stated before. Secret Societies are harder to get into than your typical Fraternity and Sorority. You will know way more friends and co-workers in a Fraternity or Sorority than in a Secret Society, true story. Fraternities and Sororities are usually for non-ivy league college students, and many can join when they first enter college. Secret Societies usually accept certain Ivy League college students by invitation only, the most advanced individuals or the most disciplined individuals, besides the family legacy clause. They're absolutely not recruiting you on Facebook and Instagram out of the blue with a long paragraph. I know you all know what I'm talking about. Look through your page inbox, "It's Right There!"

In some cases, they'll accept certain individuals who really want to serve and will commit their entire existence to it, but not just anyone. It also depends on which Secret Society it is, because some tend not to have the same entry-level expectations. Overall, Secret Societies are meant for "The Elites." "The best of the best sir," Men in Black once again. It could be said a mortal didn't even introduce the idea and the purpose of Secret Societies. The individual or beings who really run it at the very top could possibly not even be mortal at all, Men in Black. You see what I did there? I told you, "It's Right There!"

Reincarnation

Many Ancient Cultures talked about Reincarnation, and other texts have also spoken about this. As I've mentioned, souls are not being created left and right all the time, even though so much other stuff is unlimited. Reincarnation is true; if not, then Entities wouldn't even have a human experience at all. So many Ancient Cultures even believed in Reincarnation. Souls are powerful and have no one free trial type of deal. Your soul could serve its time in that one physical form, but that doesn't necessarily mean it can't serve in another physical form when called up again for duty. Souls can stick around in Spirit form as I've mentioned before, go to another physical form, or be on standby in the Spirit Realm; it all depends. The human body is just a body you use temporarily; it's not yours forever. Life and death could be so hard for people to talk about, especially if a loved one has died or is dying. We all love life, but death is a part of the cycle, too.

Fear even plays a factor with death, like losing a loved one. Having the fear of losing a loved one can be the most difficult thing for a human to live with. Imagine losing someone who meant everything to you or someone that you depended on heavily. It's hard to accept that, but you must accept losing that person and face that fear. One of the biggest tests life can give you is the death of a lover. The secret is that they will go to a calm place, will serve again in another physical form, or will still be by your side. Yes, they're no longer in that body, but the soul wasn't destroyed, and the soul is all that matters. The soul remains! Think of that person you really loved or depended on passing the torch to you, and now it's your time to carry that torch, keeping the fire lit. Sometimes you'll have to continue the journey on your own, which is life saying you are ready to lead now on your own or telling you to take that loved one's role. There's always a reason for death, even for ones closest to the heart.

In life, you must be ready for everything it throws at you because ultimately it is your own story, your own journey, and nobody else's. It wants you to be ready to rise to the occasion, overcoming anything, even pain, when the right time comes. When it comes to death, time is never in your favor. See the light in death because it's truly not the end for your loved one, nor for you. There's a light on the other side of the tunnel for you, and that loved one possibly went to a place full of light themselves. Life does go on; it doesn't stop for anyone, and you must know that by accepting it 100%.

Fear of loss is even connected to sacrifice. You could be in a scenario where you had to choose between saving your kid or saving the world. This is where fear could lead to the end of everything. The ultimate life test is choosing who you love or choosing the world. You're so conflicted with bias in this situation, being super emotional. You are aware of the world's fate but only really thinking about your kid. Logic is the last thing you're thinking about with all the emotions pouring down with this fear of loss. Fear is darkening your mind with so much force peer pressuring you to choose how you feel. It's saying, "What type of mother/father would you be if you didn't choose your kid? You know you want to save your kid. It's the only right thing to do. Go ahead and do it!" You decided to do it, and your child was saved. Listen to me clearly as I say this. "You decided to do it and your child was saved," but then you and your kid, including everyone in the whole world, died right after. The end of the world starts and ends with human's emotional drive, especially in big moments with fear being the key factor. Do you understand now? You must understand now. There's no way you can't, because "It's Right There!"

You must make sacrifices, especially in big moments! You can't be biased, you can't be super emotional, you can't be so selfish, and you must think about the long term. A decision like that labels you as an enemy against the Multiverse, must be Agent Smith or the Anti-Matter God. See, I told you, "It's Right There!" Listen everyone! Life itself, the Multiverse, your direct God if you believe in one, and others who believed in you the whole time will not leave you hanging for your huge sacrifice once again. You'll be rewarded in the grandest way ever. You become a hero by choosing to save the world, passing the test, and proving you're worthy of everything by possibly being able to lead now. Your kid isn't dead, the physical form is just no longer active. You may receive another kid or someone new in your life that becomes so special to you. This new kid or other special person in your life reminds you of the kid you lost; completely just alike. Why do you think that occurs? It occurs because that is the kid you lost. As soon as you lost your kid, the Multiverse brought that kid right back to you. The kid never really left you, the kid just changed into another physical form for you. Life does not leave you hanging for your sacrifice, it thanks you in ways that only the original "Unstoppable Force" can. It can be grand, but with a slam. Grand slam! Look at your kid! Your gift, "It's Right There!" Reincarnation!

Call of Deletion

Humans have always had the idea that the world revolves around them. That no matter what, they will always get what they want. Throughout this Multiverse, many living things have been created from Matter before human existence, and plenty more have been created after. In the real world, there's no plot armor for the people. You could be useful and/or needed until you're no longer useful or needed. The world is advancing at a fast rate. As the world advances, the people decline. Once again, if you can't keep up with the time, you'll be left behind. Anything and anyone can be replaced or abandoned to deletion if they are no longer serving a purpose. That's the number one principle throughout this Multiverse to keep a natural order of all energy and Matter. I call this the "Call of Deletion." The Call of Deletion is an activation that occurs when an existing group of Matter composed of energy gets abandoned or replaced by deletion when it no longer serves a purpose inside a Universe.

The Call of Deletion takes place when there's an error in the Cosmos, a super virus. It's no longer working. No matter how many times you reboot it, you'll end up with the same problem. You worked so hard to fix the problem and had so much data. Then you realize it's completely done for. Eventually, you'll start working on something else, throw it away, and delete every thought about it. Delete, delete, delete. Erase complete. "It's Right There!" Call of Deletion.

I believe that it happened already a long time ago, way before humans' existence. It's very likely to happen again based on Technological advancements, various readings, and my observations. It's very possible to be a Multiversal change instead of just Universal this time around. Theoretically, it would require a full override to time itself in order for it to apply instantly in every single timeline. Deletion is very calculated and usually happens instantly. To paint a picture from a visual aspect of its speed, imagine Thanos snap but with a zap instead of a slow fade. I had to use at least one Thanos snap reference for my Marvel fans. I know some may think, "This guy is crazy; it's another theory." I'm very aware of that. But the crazy thing is, the many things that I say will happen usually do happen. I'm just saying, "It's Right There." I mastered Spirituality, dug deep into Ancient History, and have admiration for the darker parts of Astronomy. Every second I spent trying to understand life.

Let me give you something you can understand. Don't get your panties caught in a wad; it's just a theory. I'm just saying, "It's Right There!"

The Fate Of the World

There are some facts in each type of Ancient Culture and Religion, with "The Bible" being one of the most powerful, well-written books in mankind. It has multiple versions with different translations. The storytelling and the many lessons that were taught for you to learn from it is truly a privilege. There's no debate about that. I'll argue about that against anyone, and I'm not even Religious. Although that statement is true, there's not one text that is 100% correct, while the others are false. It's a bit of everything, and it's all connected. It's all the same in the end. What type of end? What exactly is the end? Let me tell you if that's what you're thinking inside your head. In every Biblical text, Ancient text, and Secret Society text, the Fate of the World remains the same if the people don't change. The Fate of the World remains the same, if the people don't want to change.

Fear is indeed the biggest weapon against humans. Fear is indeed the underline for almost all their actions. Fear does affect people every single day more than any other influence in the entire world.

99% of the times, if fear gets ahold of you, that's it. People who have been oppressed become just like their oppressors because of fear. If people fear doing certain things, they'll do it even if it's the most horrible thing they can imagine. If people fear becoming something, they become it like a murderer or some sort. For a smaller example, a man could fear becoming a negatively impactful father, so he becomes a negatively impactful father or withdraws any responsibility of being a father, a non-existent one. You'll lose every time if you run away from fear instead of overcoming it by defeating it in a mental combat. You must face your fears and kill them by any means, or they will completely take control of you for all eternity to the point where it's too late to turn back. You can't run from it. Look! "It's Right There!"

Every day, people get a choice to change, but they don't. Change is too hard for them, and they will stick to what they're used to. Life gives people tests. In key moments, people fail the test; they fold because of fear. So, the Fate of the

World remains the same because the people can't change. I know it, I saw it, and I still see it because "It's Right There!"

The Power of TV

Movies and shows always foreshadowed the Fate of the World in numerous ways by Perfected ASI's being human replacements like on Westworld, I Robot, Terminator, and even on X-Men dealing with The Sentinels. Technology eventually always takes over at some point. It can always overpower a soul if it has too much energy to fight against; that's common sense. You can't stop what's already set to happen, which is the inevitable. Thanos would be so proud to hear that word so many times. Overall, movies and shows are more significant than people think. It's not just entertainment; it involves lessons and delivers subliminal messages that are very symbolic. These movies and shows aren't just all imagination; they reveal infinite numbers of possibilities of events to happen in the infinite number of timelines inside this Multiverse. You could say sometimes, they possess ideas that could be implemented in the future. Some of them occurred already in another timeline or now in another timeline.

Where did you think these writers and producers get these ideas from? So many are realistic, with some being ahead of their time predicting the future. I can't possibly be the only one who noticed that. I know you noticed it, too. It's been there the whole time. Who would have known that "It's Right There"? Television reveals it all, just like informing the people that one day the media would be bought out by billionaires, eliminating non-biased journalism. Oops! "My bad!" You didn't know? I thought you knew! I'm so sorry to hurt your feelings for that spoiler. I mean, it's not really a spoiler when they were telling you what was going to happen the whole time; that's your fault. It was on your TV screen. Look again! "It's Right There!"

The most underrated teaching in films is the Vampire scenario. Yes, we all know Vampires are considered fictional Immortals who bite all living things, especially sucking human blood to feed themselves. You don't know that there's a secret truth about it. Let me explain very clearly. Are you ready? Ready, set, go! Films are teaching you that through blood, there's a way to make you live longer and possibly become more powerful. See, usually, when Vampires bite their victims, the victim's fear impulse rises at an all-time high, causing their blood flow to surge rapidly. As the Vampires bite, the adrenaline is pumped up from both parties, and they're able to suck all the blood flow, rapidly absorbing that power from the victims' fear. In "Monsters Inc.," the Monsters were able to power up their cities through children's fear. You can absorb so much within a person's fear, and blood being involved amplifies the levels at an infinite rate out of this world.

I know what you're thinking about. I won't judge at all. Whatever people do behind closed doors to live longer or become more powerful is their business. I'm not responsible for what people do with the choices that are presented to them. They're solely responsible for anything that they've decided to do when it comes to their mortality. As long as they are serving a purpose by committing their existence to the Multiverse, I personally don't care. It's out of my hands, I'm not Allstate. I'm just saying, "It's Right There!"

If humans had a chance to live longer or become more powerful, they'll do it when tested. It's in humans' nature. For many years humans strived to find the "Fountain of Youth." You'll be surprised on the crazy things people do behind closed doors when they're thirsty needing to feed on. You heard the rumors, you saw the list, you were fully aware of the court cases. Immortality! Look! "It's Right There!" Fountain Of Youth.

So, I don't consider watching Television as a big threat to people, because you can obtain so much info to figure everything out, including people. Watching TV can be very educational, so yes it does even matter what your kids watch. Don't use TV as entertainment, use it as a lesson. Pretend you're in class when watching TV. Observe everything, and even take notes inside your head everyday like a mental note; that's Chapter 1. See, I told you, "It's Right There!"

United and Elite

There's only one race people should worry about, and that's the human race. There are bigger things that affect each and every single one of you. It doesn't matter what race you're identified as, what type of sex you are, who you sleep with or decide to love, what country you or your family are from; you all are humans. Nothing of the extra stuff really matters. You all bleed the same, so act like it. There will be some people who will read this book and say, "This was dumb and such a waste of time." Those people developed a bias after reading anything that triggered them to refuse to change, couldn't understand the information, or just simply weak. What! I'm just being honest. I'm just saying, "It's Right There."

You could give instructions on how to be a millionaire exactly step by step, and there will be plenty so eager to skip the steps, not following all the instructions provided, and then they would complain about how it didn't work for them. There will be a large portion of readers who'll think this was a great book and were interested in just hearing the knowledge but moved on, never applying anything they learned. Only a small portion, a very small percentage of readers, will apply everything that they've learned from this book. That is the reality I'm aware of. Sometimes you just can't argue with the numbers, because numbers don't lie. It's a small percentage but every percentage matters, which is the reason why I wrote, "It's Right There."

Become a part of the 1% and leave the 99% behind. Take all the responsibilities, do all that matters, and never look back. The future is secured if you make this one promise. Prophecy is Prophecy. Everything is planned, whether from Secret Societies, Entities, or the Multiverse itself. Nothing happens randomly, everything happens for a reason indeed. There may be a few paths to walk on, but all those paths were written. Walk on the right path to save yourself and others you love or who deserve to be with you. The right path is right in front of you. Start walking, "It's Right There!"

Chapter 10

Personal Human Experience

Before we go further, covering all the other aspects of this book, I want to share my experience for relatability. You can consider this Part 2 of this book, but you must get past Chapter 10 to be ready for the concluding Chapter 11; 11:11. You'll know exactly what I'm talking about after passing every level. If you want to be complete, finish P. H. E.

I will be completely honest and hold myself accountable as I know my mistakes. Sometimes, you must use yourself as an example. Some of you probably were thinking, "Who is this guy trying to tell me all of this? What's his story?" I'm totally aware of that. Everything I've experienced in this life, including my recent bond, my lives before, and my purpose, are the reasons why I am delivering this book at this exact time. I see how many people are broken today, stuck inside this loop, maze, and matrix. Listen closely as I share with you.

I was born in Queens, New York, and raised in Charlotte, North Carolina. I had 5 brothers and one sister. I remember everything I saw with my own eyes as early as an infant. In the beginning, before everything unraveled, it was just my mom and me living in that apartment above a bar, kind of like Ted and Marshall in "How I Met Your Mother." The end!

It's not exactly the end, but it's the end of the backstory. I will not put a full autobiography inside this book. This book is not about me, it's about you. Your evolution matters! I'll get straight to the point the best way I can while touching up on each Chapter dealing with me to make it all come full circle. Ready, set, go!

Signs With Me

I was able to identify the signs and understand what they all meant before I even fully understood the English language. I had strong senses at a very young age, seeing things, hearing things, and knowing things a normal person wasn't supposed to know. It was very overwhelming to feel everything so strongly and hear everything so loudly. The most significant part was I was able to see things ahead. I knew what could happen and/or what would happen, including knowing human's true dark nature. Knowing everything a person can do to me or will do to me is the reason why I wasn't talking to people in my very early years. I refused to be around or make any type of connection with people.

An everyday life is something I had to force on myself when I realized too much already. The privilege to learn without knowing was truly ruined for me very early. I received all the spoilers, indeed, and we all know everyone hates spoilers. Signs showed me my family wasn't really my family, that I lived before this one, and it also showed me who I really am/ will become. Since I forced myself to be like everyone else, I ignored many signs left and right, hoping things would turn out great. Obviously, it didn't turn out great at those times. You should not rely on hope like it's your best friend; it's not. Hope is the one person you keep in your life that disappoints you a lot, but you keep hope around because hope sometimes makes you feel better than anyone else. Stop relying on hope if you truly want or need things to work in your favor. Every sign I received was right, exactly a 100% prediction rate. When you ignore the signs that protect you from harm or inform you to accept greatness, you will always get hit and become wounded.

One time, a girl set me up many years ago during my teen years, which affected me physically, but it harmed me emotionally because I was disappointed that she initiated that. I felt it coming the day before and right before it happened, but I ignored it because I thought positively of that girl, along with the belief that it wouldn't happen to me. I was in denial of the realistic future on many other occasions. I've always thought so highly of people, so the bias was always involved. No matter how much greatness you can see in someone or in something, you must listen if your soul senses extreme danger. Your soul is the castle that protects you from invasions. It's the best line of defense to prevent any invader from entering. Your soul gives you more signs than anything else in life. Your soul is way more powerful than you have ever been taught in all your years of learning. Get to know your soul. Become one with it. So, when you hear it, listen to it. That's the key, grab the key, "It's Right There!"

My own soul was trying to protect me every day, but I've ignored it on multiple occasions. I trusted humans more than my own soul! That's why you must follow all the guides on your journey and be in sync with your intuition. The Multiverse, Spirits, and your soul are the only guides you need. The guides, your intuition, look! "It's Right There!"

Read! Reading people is something I was already great at before mastering it in human form. I've known about people mentally, emotionally, and soulfully before I continued conversing with them. Eventually, people will tell you everything about them with their actions, in case you need more data. My natural instinct is to fully observe someone scanning their whole body to upload data from them while I'm talking to them, just like an ASI. But I disciplined myself earlier on to trust people and act normally, falling through with my choices to learn like everyone else. Ignoring some signs put me in difficult places like I've mentioned before, wasting time with temporary people or users and missing out on so many phenomenal people, including grand things. Damn! I could have had a Grand slam!

Don't ignore the signs like I did for any reason; don't hold yourself back from greatness, nor put yourself in harm's way. If you do that, then you are doing it willingly. You must take accountability for anything that happens to you when ignoring signs. A sign just came. You sense it? How can you not sense it? "It's Right There!"

Fear In My Life

I personally saw how much people fear today, and even way before in the past. The number is accelerating rapidly into the future. The fears people have are being spread to others like wildfire. I've seen people fear others they don't understand, like another race or another sex, like some immature men when they see women dominate in sports that they can never dominate in themselves. I grew up around Black folks who ran away and hid things when Cops came around. Honestly, I've never had issues with Cops. You're actually better off when you don't fear them and reach out with kindness. Some people called the Cops on me for walking around using Wi-Fi, and then the Cops approached me and observed that I was not a threat at all. Fear could have made things worse for me if I had it in those moments. Fear causes suspicion and makes you more of a threat than you think you really are. Write that down; "It's Right There!" I was calm when they came around me, and nothing

119

happened because I didn't fear them; I respected them. My record was also clean, so I had zero worries. I greeted the police with respect and made/still make many connections due to that. I have a History of working with them when I was an Asset Protection Associate at Walmart and while working concerts. They are not the problem; the people who called the Cops on me out of fear are the problem.

The everyday normal citizen is more of a threat to me than the Cops are. Undisciplined people who don't commit to something involving their lives and likeness with not serving something much bigger than themselves are more to worry about than them. See what I did there? I told you, "It's Right There." How do you give a villain title to a whole group due to what a small percentage of the group does but not give the villain title to another group of people due to what a large percentage of that group does? That other group is the common people. You see, I told you, "It's Right There!" People love to deflect off themselves, even collectively, against others who are willing to do things that they didn't have the guts to do. Don't fear a certain group of people because others have that fear; assess for yourself. That's with any group, including race, sex, Religion, sexual orientation, or job title.

I Know You Want Privilege

I've seen so many wanting it better than everyone else, which is not being treated fairly but treated personally. People will skip lines, expect to not pay for something when everyone else did, and complain because they don't have it better or for simply missing out on something due to poor decision-making. I've had guests inside Walmart who would want to get high-quality customer service while stealing. There were guests at concert venues that expected refunds when they made choices to violate policies or weren't disciplined and patient enough to wait out a storm for them to attend a show after doors re-opened. Let's not forget those who come to a venue late and get upset with staff because they didn't get to see the show. Many expect to get what they want even when they are in the wrong.

I grew up with a family that steals and lies their way out of everything no matter what, even using another family member. That's all they knew how to do, no matter how much it affects another. I grew up in pre-dominantly Black neighborhoods for the most part. During my studies, I've observed that Black people were taught to use each other, to compete against one another instead of working together, and to never fully appreciate the opportunities we get every day as Americans. To rely on the past, wanting handouts, and celebrating the lack of class is what I grew up around. How can you want it better when you are not trying to be better yourself? If you want privilege, just simply be better. It's not about what you look like or what you are. It's about what you can do, who you know, and how much you know. Privilege comes with connections. Without them, you'll never get far. How do you expect to sit at the table if the people don't even know you? You can't expect to sit at the top of the table if you don't get the respect of the people at the table. So, as someone with brown skin, I made connections and thought logically about figuring out everything to stand out. I've started from the bottom and risen to the top. I shall keep rising at that.

A system can only exist if everyone is still doing all the work to keep it working. You can't blame the system. The system needs people. If the people keep doing the same thing, then how do you expect the system to change? Break the system! Nobody is going to save you with something you must figure out on your own. No one is going to make the necessary changes for you; change is not going to just happen for you, change is within you. You are in control of the changes. If you can't change, nothing will change. If you truly are superior as you say you are, then show it. If you change, you're out of the system and the system will no longer work. Just like I've recently said, "The system needs people." See, I told you, "It's Right There!"

The secret about that is that the system only exists because it exists inside your head. You let it linger right there! It's not real; you only tell yourself that and make it a reality by manifesting it. That's why it's not beneficial to have negative thoughts and think that everything is against you, when it's really you against you with that fear you have. I know some people right now will say, "hmm, I never thought about it like that." Well, you know now. "It's Right There!" Positivity is key, grab the key, "It's Right There!"

If you want something, you get it. If you have a problem with something, be better positioned to change it. Stop complaining! Stop blaming! Victim mentality is weak. The famous saying, "Do something about it." There's no excuse why you can't have it better. That drive, that ambition, that understanding will take you places. It will take you anywhere, everywhere! That privilege you seek is near, "It's Right There!"

Change With America

Change is the same with America. This is a message to all my fellow Americans, a public service announcement. If you hate America, then that's a form of self-hate because you are American. If you have a problem with America, then you have a problem with yourself. America is within you, it's what you make it out to be. America is one of the greatest countries in the world. People come here to live the "American Dream." Within 3 years, they could be living that dream. People come here with absolutely nothing, then end up with so much in return, providing generational wealth for their family. Now that's what I call The American Dream, "It's Right There!"

This country has opportunities for everyone to thrive, no matter what country you're originally from or your skin color. There are so many opportunities that are not in other countries. People come here because they can thrive better than other countries, especially their former country. Why do you think they came here? The American Dream. You see, I told you, "It's Right There!" Their country wasn't like America, so they wanted to be American. Appreciate being American. It's not the United States of America unless we're all united. United and Elite! You see, I told you, "It's Right There!"

You can't rely on the past when every day you get a chance to make History and reshape your future, including your people's future. Also, if it didn't affect you directly, then you are choosing to upset and limit yourself. People who talk negatively about the country are mostly upset with what's happening in their lives. People who don't talk negatively about their country usually love everything going on in their lives or take accountability when it's not going their way. This country isn't perfect, and no country is perfect. We can compare all day, but living here every single day with the chance to change the tides of the ocean is worth it. The ocean is your life. Your life is worth it!

"Land of the Free" really means the land to be all you can be, along with being free. The real free, not the brainwashed free I've stated in Chapter 2. That refers to your unlimited capabilities and the unlimited energy you can absorb to power you to live an extravagant life in your infinite evolution. Being a real American means no longer being controlled and becoming superior. You'll never be free if you're always in a victim's mindset and not growing to capitalize on opening the many doors that you never knew existed. If you can't be free in this land, then you'll never be free in any land. "This land is your land, this land is my land, from California to the New York Island." Don't just sing it, know it! Are you ready to be a true American? The door that you know now exists is there. "It's Right There!"

Emotional Drive Personal Observation

My mother in this life was very emotionally driven and lacked plenty of emotional intelligence, honestly. Her every frustration was taken out on me and my siblings, but mostly me. Some always wondered why. Whatever she felt like saying or doing, she did it. The fear, the defensive mechanisms that were mostly offensive, and the stress were obvious throughout the many years of observing her. I've received so much data on humans in my studies because of her. She had a fear of me outgrowing the poor lifestyle mentally and financially, along with the fear of me not having a relationship with her in the future. She managed to say and do everything to make that fear happen. When you're always deflecting off yourself and mentally abusing someone by using them at times, the probability of that person leaving is 99 to 1. There's a 99% chance of that happening.

I've often heard the accusation, "You think you're better than everyone," but it's a claim I never made during my childhood. Similarly, I've been labeled as selfish, despite my track record as a team player, a people pleaser, consistently at someone's service, and frequently sacrificing my own plans for others. Interestingly, her fears turned out to be projections of her own behavior.

What I've come to understand is that she was the one displaying selfishness. For instance, she became upset when I declined to put my name down for a house that wouldn't even be mine, given her poor credit History in 2019. Moreover, she actively discouraged me from pursuing higher education, urging me to prioritize financial assistance for her instead of my own dreams. This was particularly detrimental in my graduation year of 2015 when I missed out on opportunities that could have propelled my music career. For many years, she had always mentioned, "I need help to get back on my feet," but she never tried to get back on her feet. I never even had a chance to get on my feet as soon as I turned 18 in 2015 to start my life and accomplish my goals like a young adult is supposed to. She also took care of her sexual needs with her young boyfriends instead of cooking food for her own kids when they needed dinner throughout my pre-teen and teen years.

I've learned that when people say that 'better' line, it's because you show you are better and that you deserve so much more, striving to be better every day, and they can't stand that. It taught me people will be jealous because they see you can do better, are more disciplined, and are willing to have more class than them. It shows you want to grow, while that person basically tells you it's hard for them to grow. People will try to hold you back and believe that you are not a great person when you have all the potential to be so. These emotionally driven people want you on their level or beneath you. They don't want to see you blossom. If you do blossom, they will want all the credit just because they feel entitled. I'm grateful because it made me who I am today. Let people show you who they are, be patient, and know when to move. Appreciate even all the negative things you receive from people. A soul is a soul, people are people, and if someone isn't positively significant to you, then you must let them go. Word is bond. Time is everything. Those are keys. Grab the keys, by the door. "It's Right There!" Slam the door! You shall see me, no more. 3!

Another super emotionally driven person was the only person I connected with soulfully. It was like she hated many things and hated almost everyone due to her past. The fear within her was so deep, and I've tried to get it out of her. She had many moments of tears pouring down in extreme sadness and moments of extreme madness. The outbursts were difficult to watch sometimes. Any time she had a high impulse of anger, she would make very emotional decisions no matter what. It doesn't matter how it would affect her or me or anyone she cares about after; she's going to do it regardless. When she has that emotional drive-in key moments, there's no stopping her from causing future harm. You could reason with her and inform her about exactly what would happen with a clear mind of logic; she wouldn't listen even if you were right. So many "fuck it" decisions were made. When someone is so emotional that they block out all voices and ignore any advice, that's very dangerous.

She would make a mistake repeatedly, putting herself in harmful situations, and some could even be prevented if she communicated and didn't hide crucial info. Eventually, that emotional drive came to bite me in my ass later and eroded me completely like a meteor crashing into my heart, mind, and soul. Everything she hated people for doing that she said was super trifling, she did it herself. Everything she feared becoming, she became. The dark cloud took over and wreaked havoc, and she let it take over willingly. That emotional drive made her lose everything she loved, including me, and it killed all the things that made her special and stand out from the rest positively. Those short-term emotional decisions affected her future self, her image, and she descended as a soul preventing her evolution. I have never seen someone that emotionally driven in my entire existence.

Seeing someone fall completely off after receiving so much guidance, patience, unconditional love, and forgiveness for many actions was brand new to me. It's more significant and hits differently when it's someone closest to you. She had the highest potential I'd ever seen but failed in the biggest moments when she was tested. The signs told me it was going to happen, and I knew closer to that time that it would happen, and I saw it right before it happened. There it goes; "It's Right There." I can't even stop the inevitable. It was a full self-sabotage, and fear consumed her 100% to the point where she couldn't even trust herself. Everything I've witnessed with this woman gave me the biggest data ever. It made me see how much fear is within humans and the control it has on humans to the point of breaking them. I couldn't write "It's Right There" if I didn't go through that. My feelings, my time, and my pre-soul tie were sacrificed to create this book. I needed to see, hear, and feel the meteor at full strength when I wasn't ready for it. I am now able to help people with their fears because of it, so I am not mad at all. There's no hate in my heart. I understand, sometimes you can't save everyone, not even from themselves. I had to see how extreme it was, and I needed to get knocked on my ass because of it.

First Encounters and The Fear I Once Had

I've noticed when some people meet me or even a little after, they get scared because I'm too different. I sense the fear 100% every time I read them. They may think I'm so-called "too good" for them to accept due to their personal issues, too unreadable and possibly be future harm, or think I truly don't exist like a walking myth, as I said before. People's trauma from the past or fear of hurting me or hurting them is an eater. I have a theory that some women's souls sense my power level within my Ancient soul, and they instantly get that fear and pull away. A strong presence that's unrecognizable in current times can always give rise to a fear impulse. Logically, I can't complain about it, and Spiritually, I do understand. I also have a theory that people recognized I was reading them while talking to them, which may have rubbed them off the wrong way, so it was a disadvantage.

Sometimes, I detected their energy and approached them based on the energy they transferred to me. I'm aware of certain things that may be pros internally but are cons externally. I've realized that I put people on such a high pedestal, so seeing someone who looks at them like they're so amazing or Godly scares them. The pressure people feel because they don't think they're that great made me realize how much people don't believe in themselves. The high pedestal only puts them in a position of having to be better or simply match that energy, which many feel they can't do consistently. "She wasn't ready," Kevin Hart.

It's possible that someone from the past may have treated them kindly or viewed them in a positive light, only to hurt that person eventually. The challenging aspect of the fears people harbor about me, whether rooted in past experiences or concerns about the future, is that it consistently left me feeling deeply disappointed. This disappointment created a lingering negativity that affected me personally for years. As many would aptly put it today, "It really sucks." There have been numerous individuals whom I genuinely believed had great potential. I desired to see them realize that potential and become someone special in their lives, irrespective of any formal titles. It's disheartening to envision greatness in others only to discover that they harbor negative thoughts about me. What compounded the hurt was that, more often than not, I never had the chance to showcase my abilities or demonstrate the person I could be to them.

I strongly adhere to the principle of Acts of Service, meaning I'm committed to serving and being of importance to others. This extends to being a man of my word, where I make a conscious effort to ensure that my actions consistently align with my words.

My biggest fear growing up was ending up alone, meaning no wife or kids. I was once emotionally driven myself because of this fear. This is what I was referring to when I meant the buildup that negatively affected me. I promise to explain more about that in Parts 3, 4, and 6 after this. It made me very desperate to love, even clingy at times. I've always known I would one day achieve all my career goals, have grand health and wealth, but it wouldn't matter much to me if I didn't have my own family. I could be wealthy and have all the power in the world, but that would have never satisfied me.

I wanted to love and have a normal life like every other human. Love was the one thing that I looked forward to having in this life. I was always running away from that fear early on in my years and never came to terms with defeating that fear for so long. The truth is, I've been seeing the future of that happening since I was a kid, and from time to time, I still had visions of it as I grew older. The thing about that is it's nothing to fear because, before this life, I'd never had that anyway. Based on that, why should I fear when I've gone through that before with no problem? I learned that I've made it into a fear when it's just a realistic reality that's not brand new, which I must be ok with. I faced that fear I had implanted inside my brain. This fear had me holding on to people who weren't soulful for the long run and wouldn't go where I was going. This fear was keeping me away from my true destiny, restricting me from greatness, including success, grand health, and wealth. This fear was against everything I ever stood for.

I shall fear no more. I shall not hold myself back anymore. I shall not even think about a fear on me ever again. I am fearless! I am ready to walk only forward and not backward! I am an "Unstoppable Force"! Fear is lying down on the ground in defeat. Look! "It's Right There!" My role on this Earth requires focus and sacrifices of any wants, etc. I must not let a craving or a powerful opposing force control me. When you really want something, you set yourself up in a trap and can develop a fear. Don't take the bait! Meet all the requirements that are asked of you and set your desires on fire. You must accept prophecy, do what you need to do on Earth, and let the chips fall where they may. If it's not meant for me in this life, then it's not meant to be. We all must respect the path and certain tasks that were chosen for us.

Regarding that fear of not having my own family, my life can still be a grand slam without one. No matter what I look forward to having in this life, bigger things that don't require my feelings are at stake. The fate was written before my feelings existed. Prophecy! Yes, I mentioned these laws and amendments existed before your feelings existed, but my fate existed before those laws and amendments existed. Let's try again. The fate was written before my feelings existed. Prophecy! The right person to build a family will be there whenever it's supposed to be. I must not rely heavily on it, because, according to the schedule, I've got bigger things to attend to. My future success, unlimited evolution, and completion of my role on Earth are there. "It's Right There!"

Communicate With Me

Personally, I've never been inclined to communicate through the phone; I've engaged in it primarily for the sake of others. Despite my reluctance, I fulfilled the necessary communication without personal interest. In today's communication landscape, I'm a complete outsider. To be candid, I find it challenging to align with how people commonly communicate nowadays. I've observed that maintaining open, honest, and detailed communication— speaking one's mind and avoiding time-wasting small talk—doesn't resonate with at least 70% of people today. It's a true story. I've never been a fan of small talk; I love to talk about the deep stuff and all the important things in life, but most people like to be distracted and not focus on the important things in life. The materialistic individuals are the ones who have a distaste for deep conversations. Old souls barely fit in today's world, especially if you're a young adult with old-school communicative ways. Ancient souls don't fit in today's world at all and are super rare to find with the many centuries that existed in this Multiverse.

There were times I would get someone's phone number and send a nice respectful message informing them of my intentions, looking forward to getting to know someone, but most of the time, that didn't end up great. I've learned with people my age and younger that it's weird to them. They're not used to talking to a gentleman or don't like formal behavior. I realized that people are not about what they say because most are "in the moment" people. They do and say things in the moment without being ready to follow up. While they may feel and think a certain way when you first meet them, they soon recognize that they lack the capability or commitment for proper communication. They can tell with your first message. They see it, "It's Right There!" They talked an exceptional game with so much excitement but couldn't properly follow up. As Kevin Hart puts it, "She wasn't ready."

It can be confusing why some women prefer a guy to wait an extended period before texting them after exchanging numbers, instead of someone like me who wastes no time in communicating, showing I'm serious and true to my word. Whether it's days or weeks, they seem to appreciate that approach, but why? If a guy waits so long, he isn't genuinely interested in talking or building a bond. This is why I asked that question. How people communicate, and their words reveal a lot about them. I've always disliked Language Arts, being one of those students who says, "I already know how to read and write." Later, I realized the crucial nature of Language Arts because mastering it is needed in everyday communication. Year after year, you'll be conditioned to sharpen your comprehension skills, which is never a waste of time. EOG/EOC tests or any other tests train you to highlight keywords and underline sentences. Highlighting keywords and underlining sentences will help you understand what a person is saying in every sentence.

I personally kept doing that not only through written form, but verbally when people speak. You'll pick up everything someone tells you verbally and in written form. That's why it is important to read and listen; you will miss out on revealing things if you don't. Assumptive language, suggestive language, call to action, tones, verb tenses, and everyone's motives you will be able to identify with perfect comprehension skills. I tell you, I want to get to know you. I tell you that you seem amazing because you seemed amazing. I tell you I want to hang with you, so we can get comfortable around each other in person like people should. Playing phone tap with texting back-to-back without seeing each other in a close-mile radius is childish. Waiting forever for a text back here and there consecutively for days without scheduling a date, planning to talk in person, or even scheduling a phone call is also pointless.

For centuries, souls have bonded the most through talking in person, even if someone else had to communicate for them on their behalf when restricted to do so. For so many centuries since the beginning of humanity, people only sent letters delivered by people or Creatures when located very far away from them. In some cases, messages were communicated through forms of rituals with heavy Symbolism. I want someone to read my body language, identify my tone, sense my energy, and make eye contact with me as a sign of respect. I am trying to establish mutual respect and hide nothing from another. I want to reveal all of me, and having the same in return makes sense. The natural way is the way I've always tried to be. I listen to people, I'm confident in my speaking, I'm comfortable in my own skin around people, and I want people to be comfortable speaking freely to or around me.

I never try to waste anybody's time. When communicating, I strive to treat people how I would want to be treated. How can we know each other if we never ask the right questions about each other? How can we understand each other if we never have deep conversations? How can we ever truly be comfortable with each other if we never spend true quality time with each other without the extra stuff? You can't; that's why you got caught off guard finding out something about that guy you were dating and didn't even know. See, I told you, It's Right There"!

When I inquire about your thoughts, it's an indication that your opinions matter to me, and I value your mentality. Similarly, when I ask how you feel about something, it's a signal that I genuinely care about your emotions—what triggers you, your preferences, and dislikes are crucial for me to understand. This knowledge is essential for providing meaningful assistance and support. Conversely, if someone never asks about your thoughts or feelings, it implies that these aspects don't hold significance for them. Essentially, they communicate that your feelings and thoughts are not a priority in their eyes. A friend of mine once mentioned that she had never come across this perspective before. As I mentioned before, "It's Right There!"

People are too accustomed to being around and talking to people who don't care about them or care what they think, which includes never really listening to them. So don't ever get annoyed if someone asks for your response to something they said; they're trying to include you in things and ultimately telling you that you will always be considered. I am considerate, and it's a pro and a con. The pros and cons depend on the type of person I've come across. Listening is something I disciplined myself to do. My ears weren't always the best at hearing, but I focused to really listen to what I heard. Sometimes, I would replay the sounds or words in my head to assess it further. You could do a sales pitch or promote your Religion on me, I would still allow you to get your words and finish as I look at you and listen. Respect!

I know a person could maybe say something I needed to hear in that moment. It could be new info or a reminder, or it could mean a lot to that person for me just listening to them. You never know unless you listen. I've spoken to many people in different countries from different backgrounds and races in the world, and I've learned so much about these places and more about those people because of them. You can become more skilled as a talker and as a listener by having these conversations. You can never learn or get better at listening if you don't try, and you can never learn or get better at speaking if you're not actively speaking. I've come across multiple people online who had social anxiety or didn't like their voice and/or couldn't speak well.

In school, they condition you to present PowerPoints in front of classmates, do speeches in front of classmates, and work side by side with classmates in small groups. They do that to help you socialize, learn how to work with others to achieve a certain task, and perfect your speaking skills to speak comfortably in front of an audience. If you ever want to be a leader or become the CEO of a company, then you must know how to speak to people with a full understanding of teamwork. If you want to make a lot of money and do business, then you will have to put yourself out there daily to speak. Networking is key, grab the key, "It's Right There!"

Proper communication is how conflicts like war are ended. Proper communication is how deals are made. Proper communication is how you solve an infinite number of problems. You can't move forward without communication. Communication is essential in life indeed. It's a reason why Language Arts and Math go hand-in-hand when it comes to the importance of a subject, even regarding communication. You got the Math, which is your logical thinking that comes up with solutions, but now you need to communicate in some type of language to solve the problems with the solutions you have. You see what I did there? I told you, "It's Right There!" Remember, I started off not speaking to people, then started speaking to multiple people, and now I am speaking to masses at one time. See, I told you,

"It's Right There." Anyone who has a voice to use can properly speak and listen. The proof is there, "It's Right There."

Sometimes, being too communicative can be an issue, especially if there are high impulses of emotion involved. I know all about this, as I was completely guilty. I have been emotionally driven even when it came to communication. I used to over-text and be impatient at times when texting. The high impulses of sadness or anger, in general, made me call or text an individual consecutively in a small-time frame. You appear toxic or can be considered toxic with the way you communicate. After everything, I've learned there's no need to be impatient or overreact. I had to master patience and control my emotions involving another in communication. If someone doesn't give a fuck, then I shouldn't give a fuck. I myself can't get upset if someone doesn't properly communicate with me, nor do I need to express how upset I am with that high impulse.

I realized that people were doing me a favor. So, if someone can't properly communicate with me, then there's no need to keep communicating with them, or chase them. If someone is hiding too much, they can't be trusted. If someone does something very atrocious, there is no need to waste my energy on it. If you're full of fear, stay your ass, right there! If people don't like me, then I shouldn't get upset, nor get so defensive asking them why they don't like me. I shouldn't let it get to me. Candace Owens once said, "Life's tough, get a helmet man." I love that line, and I replay that clip all the time. It was such a badass moment, especially how she served that platter and went to the very next individual to serve. It must have been a busy night at the restaurant. That serve had so much power, speed, and precision. You would think she was a tennis player. One set, to the very next set, to the very last set. Damn! It was grand, but with a slam. Grand slam! I've become the master of letting people disqualify themselves for me. Let people disqualify themselves for you. That's the key, grab the key, "It's Right There!"

What's the point of building a connection or partnership if we can't properly communicate? I should be able to call you or video chat with you. Yes, I send messages saying everything I need to say or may sound very passionate about how I express my words, and it may be some paragraphs. There's nothing wrong with that. You can feel free to type me paragraphs with being completely honest and transparent no matter what, even to disconnect. Yes, I read; I don't skim. I'm not sorry that I'm not a texter; I'm an author. You should obviously know that by now. I mean, look at these Chapters, look at these pages, look at these words. "It's Right There!"

My Love and Lust History

Lust

Let me start off with Lust. I've hated lusting. If I was a lawmaker right now, I'd ban porn. Delete, delete, delete. Erase complete. Lust filled my mind, heart, and soul so many times. The urge to ejaculate always disgusted me. I can admit I sent and received pics, videos, and had sexual conversations with people. In the social media era where everyone reacts quickly, making "fuck it" decisions with their high impulses of lust and more, it's not surprising, especially as a teenage boy or young adult male. I wasn't perfect, and I was being an undisciplined human who was broken; that's the truth. That same lack of discipline due to lust and being broken had me even harassing some people via phone with people I lusted over or didn't like anymore but contacted them just because I was lonely.

No matter how much I lusted, I didn't want to sexually meet up with 87% of the people I sexually talked to. I hoped I was never in the same room with most of those people, and I am glad life prevented it. Honestly, I never would've engaged in conversation with about 24% of them in person. There are reasons why my sexual body count didn't exceed past my hands. You'll be surprised by how many people my age and younger, sexual body count passed their hands. What! I'm just saying, "It's Right There!" I was mostly all talk, honestly. Many people have diseases, have illegitimate children from sex, and other negative effects that occur from casually having sex with people, especially with the wrong people.

Lust made me damage my skin in my private area as a long-term effect due to my consistent physical activity of friction to release my fluids. I always felt so uncomfortable and made some others feel uncomfortable after releasing my fluids from the high impulse of lust. Embarrassed and ashamed of myself are exactly the words to describe it, because logically I needed to be in control of it. The lack of discipline in fighting against lust frustrated me, but lust is a powerful force.

I've engaged in intimate relationships with individuals who didn't meet my personal standards, and the experience of having sex with someone I wasn't in a committed relationship with always left my soul feeling uneasy. Sex is a soul exchange, so it should be shared with someone you generally love. The person you love, should be your wife or husband.

Reflecting on my past choices, I find myself wishing I had remained a virgin, persevering that sacred moment with my wife. I can imagine it now; it's there, "It's Right There." But a simple daydream of imagination on what I cannot undo, can't become a reality, and that's why we must not heavily weigh on the things we can't change. Admitting to a lapse in commitment, I acknowledge succumbing to lust as a distraction from life's challenges, ultimately facing the consequences. Excessive lust led me to be attracted to individuals I wouldn't find appealing under normal circumstances — many are quite unattractive if you look past the sexual factors. What! I'm just saying, "It's Right There!"

I grew up where male family figures watched porn, and I was exposed to it at a very young age. I was taught how to have sex with girls, as a very little boy, from my oldest brother. Throughout the years, I've had cousins and a brother who had sex with many women and even brought them home sometimes. These people had a lot of one-night stands. Many guys growing up always talked about having sex with multiple women and watching porn flicks. It's not essential for society if young men grow up with the idea that having sex with multiple women is cool. Porn watching among young men should be discouraged. If you think about it, it's very strange and un-natural for men or even women to enjoy other people having sex with each other. Sex should be private, between the parties behind closed doors. It's a reason why "do not disturb" signs are on doors at hotels and other places with couples involved, which are usually placed on doors right before sex. See, I told you, "It's Right There!"

After my last bond with the woman that I soulfully connected with, it made me see how much lust has control over people today. I grew a distaste for sex realizing I must break free from it completely. I needed to see it up close, controlling someone I deeply loved, to understand the danger of it fully. I'm forever grateful for the lessons on why lust is so harmful to people's minds, hearts, and souls.

I'm on a no-lust journey, and I have never been better in my life. I am better off without it. I don't need sex, and I'll be fine never to have it again, nor have a sexual conversation again. To not think about it nor watch anything sexual, including not looking at someone in a sexual way, is truly amazing. I can see people for what they truly are; the real things only matter to me. If you can't go without sex being unmarried, then you are showing me that you are weak. You just disqualified yourself for me. It's easier to hold my standards up, and my standards have risen because of everything I've gone through. I am no longer weak for lust. I defeated it! The freedom from lust is the best freedom that people never thought of, or pictured. Think about it and visualize it now. You see it? How can you not see it? "It's Right There!"

My Mother's Love Influence

Growing up, I've never been taught how to properly love or informed on how crucial it is to build a family. My mother had had seven kids with four guys before she turned 27. My father wasn't active for most of my life, but I did have an active father in the household who was my stepfather from age 4 to 11. I never fully appreciated him as my stepfather until after. He always taught us stuff, supported our talents, and ensured we went to school every day and did our homework. I've watched how my mother ended her marriage with him; it was very messy. She started having an affair with one of my cousins' best friends. That's when she started to get exposed from a lover standpoint and from a family standpoint. Since then, she dated and had sexual relations with younger men, including friends of my oldest brother and cousins. She got into situations young women usually get themselves into. She always chose guys who weren't mentally or emotionally outstanding. She never considered choosing a man that was soulful for her in the long run or pleasant to have around your kids. When you have a partner, you must think about your kids; that's the most important part. Your kids will always come first! They are from you and are the future! A man who is not even your husband shouldn't have received more love than the love you give your kids. She personally expressed her preference of not wanting men of high caliber, reflecting that she hasn't matured enough to become better and attract better. We all know you are what you attract; that's Dating 101. It was like she feared getting older with the behavior to develop relations with younger men, and she attacked responsibilities less due to that fear. Her having kids as a young teenager was a key factor because it disabled her from living life like a normal teenager.

It's kind of surprising, because my grandparents have been together since they were teenagers, creating seven kids together. Based on that, she had a proper example of building a family when you choose a lifelong partner. The most shocking thing is that she never encouraged any of us to become real men. Let me explain that more. She urged us not to care much about these women and let them chase us, nor do anything significant for them. She let my oldest brother bring women over, just so he can have sex with them many times; not trying to push him to become a better man. It all happened inside her household for years and years, including not making sure the home looked presentable consistently, which other parents made sure of in my experiences visiting another's home.

Speaking of pushing, I've wished my mother had pushed me to success, to never settle for mediocrity just like other parents did with their kids. I've seen parents get upset if their son or daughter got a C on their grades, and I was so surprised to know that. Knowing that made me want that. I needed to be pushed academically and have a parent who wanted me to be very ambitious, caring about my future 100%. Challenges are how people grow and define their greatness. Those parents want their kids to be the best and have a better life than they did. Out of all my siblings, I was the only one who completely changed my surroundings. I was super ambitious and pushed myself to improve every day. That statement still applies today. If you truly care about your kid's success, you must pay attention to them and guide them to higher their standards. That's mentally, emotionally, and soulfully when it comes to standards. So, if you can't do that, then that's why you should choose a great man who can be a great father to do that for you. This is why you need a full household with a mother and father. You see, I told you, "It's Right There!"

My mother had an issue with me and my other siblings having a girlfriend more than just having sex with a woman. That's very absurd, and every woman should be shaking their head hearing that. Whenever I had a girlfriend, she always had an issue with me showing love to them and taking care of them, but that's what I was supposed to do as a man. She had an issue due to a fear of being replaced with me loving another woman more than her, and it's more of a deflection on her decision to choose men who doesn't do the same for her. I've heard, "You don't tell me that you love me like that, but I bet you always tell your girl that you love her." Her teachings and behavior can create a toxic man for many women to have issues with, which I mentioned before on how parents create toxic lovers in Chapter 4.

I had to learn how to choose the right woman and discipline myself to become a man. It was very crucial, especially during my teen years with her thinking and without that active father figure inside the household. My grandfather was a great example as he served in the military and always pushed his emotions to the side. He sacrificed for his family for many years, including driving many family members to work at a very old age. Two of my uncles were also great examples and were very strong about keeping a household together. You must master emotional intelligence, challenge your kids in every way, and prepare them for the world like being a wife or husband one day as a parent. I've said this before, "It's Right There!" It's your duty as a parent, and as a server of the Multiverse. When it comes to a kid, your feelings don't matter, the future matters, which is your kid. Your kid! Look! "It's Right There!"

Sucker For Love

I honestly can go on forever talking about the love part of my life, but I must keep it simple. I always loved hard, wanting to be that special someone, hoping things could last forever. Yes, that's true, but I was once broken and been more emotional at times than I should have for many years. Almost everyone has, that's a fact. We all must grow stronger, become more logical, kill the victim mentality, and not rely on the feelings from the past. That's the key, grab the key, "It's Right There!"

Now it's time to dig deep into my love life without the family's influence, etc. As I've mentioned with the fear I had, I strived to be with someone I could call mine for life. I fell in love too many times. It really was infatuation, especially as a teenager and as a young adult. So many women seemed amazing to me already, or possibly could be super amazing due to the potential that I saw in them. They never reached it, and many of the human population today won't live up to their potential. I've always thought I could work it out with this and that person or try to be the knight in shining armor to someone who needed real love. I've learned it doesn't work out in the end, especially in this generation. Never try to save someone who hasn't healed yet! I hoped so many times to get it right.

I was like Ted Mosby on "How I Met Your Mother." I've been the type to like one person and never got paid attention to, or been friend-zoned, or didn't get a real chance. Ted Mosby! The AI that spoke my lines to me while editing this book even sounds like Ted Mosby. See, I told you, "It's Right There!" Ted Mosby! I wasn't exactly Ted Mosby, because I had the confidence of Barney Stinson. It was just a couple of differences. I possessed great speaking skills, knew how to approach a woman in person, and wasn't looking for one-night stands. My in-person ratio was way better. What! I'm just saying, "It's Right There!"

If you're unfamiliar with "Barney Stinson," he was another character on "How I Met Your Mother," who was a suit-and-tie guy who always flirted with women at bars in many creative ways to have one-night stands with them. If you love comedy, then you must watch it. I highly suggest you follow up by watching "The Big Bang Theory" and "Young Sheldon." Search it up! Look! "It's Right There!" I never took breaks from having conversations with women. Some I've wanted to be friends with because I felt more comfortable around women and expressing my feelings honestly, along with wanting to guide them on becoming powerful. I discussed love, some genres of music like Pop music, and other things I can't discuss with a guy.

Most guys do talk about the same things and hide a lot within when around other men, while women reveal so much. I caught feelings for some of those friends, even hoping I could be next up to date after their relationship, just like Ted Mosby with Robin numerous times. That damn Robin! If you know, you know. "It's Right There!" I know what it's like never to take the proper time to heal and work on the issues to become better in order to receive better. I've had a victim mentality installed in my brain while also not taking accountability on numerous occasions. I chose to put myself in certain positions, including the people I chose. The choice was there, "It's Right There!"

The One Who Changed My Life Twice

I finally took a break and healed, refocusing only on my purpose, but then I met someone who caught my soul's attention. I must repeat some lines that I've stated before. Please don't feel annoyed with me saying them again. Are you ready? I honestly didn't want to write this part as I've grown stronger, become more logical, killed the victim mentality, and don't rely on the feelings from the past. It's basically bringing up old feelings and thoughts, along with walking you through it moment by moment. Regardless, it doesn't matter what I want to do, it's about what I need to do. I must tell you because it's the best way to help you. I could not have revealed anything at all and erased this whole Chapter, but I owe it to you and everyone else. There's always a time when things that are kept in the dark must be seen in the light. You can never grow unless what which you hide, receives some sunlight. That applies to everything. I will not reveal every detail out of respect and to give this person some privacy, as I have no hate towards this person. However, I must talk about this connection in order to relate properly.

I relocated states for this bond, and sacrificed a lot to make this bond work. I did use the 3 methods before making that decision, but I should have listened to the signs more than my logical thinking and observation of the actions in the present. The signs spoke louder than anything, and emitted unprecedented soundwaves. I was a knight in shining armor saving the damsel in distress, which she always said by the record. There was a lot I wasn't aware of coming into the relationship, and sometime after, it showed red flags of signs that I ignored. Despite that, I still stuck around because this person was so different than everyone else. She even looked at me in a way that was different than everyone else. I had many deep, long conversations with this woman, including Spiritual ones. We were both Spiritually aligned, and she wanted to learn more. The compatibility was there for the long-term, including raising our kids about 96% the same way. I've told her so many things, even secrets about me. I don't celebrate holidays or even my own birthday, but I've done things for her on days that are important to her, like her birthday. I never did, nor do anything like that for anyone.

She had certain values that many women of today lacked. I respected her very much and never asked for sexual content via phone, nor had sexual conversations with her throughout the years. She was naturally a healer and had the highest potential that I've ever seen in all my existence, which I've mentioned before. I've already mentioned her emotional drive, which caused her to make mistakes and not listen. That was after and way before the biggest heartbreak I've received, but I wasn't innocent either. Over time, those actions frustrated me and caused me to do some immature things. I had some conversations with people, some that were distasteful that she saw. Some I expressed as it weren't a big deal, but it was to her. I'd started to lack some emotional intelligence due to the buildup of the lack of listening and sabotages. It did get to me, though at times it felt like it didn't. Those were the first steps of denial. Men deny the things that frustrate them more than anyone else at times, and it causes them to react unpleasantly.

I cared about this woman and her growth, so I've always pushed her to be at her very best to grow mentally, emotionally, and even financially. No matter what happened in the past with her, I've strived to help her out. A team is how I viewed us, so I had to be the man and lead. I took the initiative, assuming my role 100%, paying most of the household expenses, including making every sacrifice I needed to ensure my woman was set. She made this one huge mistake later that could have been prevented through communication, which made me sacrifice again. It was a huge one because I was on my way to doing something I'd wanted to do for years. It could have put me ahead career-wise. I honestly was fed up with this one to the point where I wanted to break it off completely this time. I've thought about breaking it off a couple of times in the past due to these sabotages, because each one was crucially affecting her and us as a team negatively.

I decided to keep it going, but shortly after, I made a "fuck it" decision due to that high impulse of frustration and due to me keeping my word to another person. Oh yeah! Another con about me is that I always keep my word on favors, highly guilty. But yes, I've physically cheated on her with a friend. I did, and I wasn't proud of it. I regretted it right after. I knew it wasn't for me, and it sure wasn't something to boast about like a typical guy would. Having full sexual contact with someone other than the one I loved did not sit right with my soul. My soul fucking hated me! My mind hated me! My heart hated me! That's 3, and all you need is 3; "It's Right There!"

About a week later, it was making me sick. I couldn't keep it from her. Eventually, I told her, and it fucking crushed her. I felt like her worst nightmare when I told her that. I thought it was over and that I really messed it up. It did affect her for days. She forgave me after thinking about it and receiving some advice from a male boss at her job. She didn't have to forgive me, but she did. I was grateful and was willing to marry her even right after to commit fully, but we eventually agreed to have a proper wedding instead. Based on that, I decided to wait it out. Eventually, I told someone who was considered my best friend at the time, and she told me that she would never have informed her partner willingly like that. That's very shocking to hear that from a woman's mouth, and I did say women hide things better than men in Chapter 4. Watch out! I'm just saying, "It's Right There!"

Many months passed by, and it became a new year. During this new year, she introduced a new friend who was a guy. I'd never met the man that she started to text or met him in the aftermath of everything. The way she introduced him with the certain details she expressed and mixed with the instant jump in her body language, I knew it was going to be something that would bite me in the ass later. I knew because of the signs, because of my History of being a male friend in the past, and along with past lovers who had a male friend they eventually messed around with. I trusted her because she was my partner, due to my past big mistake, and her reactions when she heard or saw people do hurtful things to a lover, whether in real life or fictionally through TV. Her reactions after observing flagrant behavior are the main reason why I felt more comfortable trusting her.

Some months after, I told on myself about when I was going to propose due to my influence of being high from taking a THC edible. So, I had to change my plans and make it sooner to catch her off guard. I did catch her off guard and proposed. My legs were shaking so much, and I had never been so nervous as I was in that moment. A man is most vulnerable when he proposes and when he's at his wedding watching his fiancé walk down the aisle. She was crying and eventually said yes. My lover was extremely happy, and we celebrated the next day at a free concert at a music venue where I worked. She was so happy to be a fiancé and bragged about it so much. One of her goals since a kid was to be with someone who took her seriously enough to marry her. I was happy to see her happy, even showing her off to coworkers and female friends. I bragged about how amazing she was to everyone and even showed pictures of her or us.

Since I was engaged, I had to really think about the future. I had to make a career change. I wanted to be able to pay for the wedding and honeymoon, which would have been in Egypt, and have a nice career to build a successful, happy family. The goal was to ensure I could be the husband to financially take care of everything and give her all she wanted. One day at this new job, she was at that guy friend's house I had never met. From what I was aware of, it was even her first time meeting him, meaning it was a long-distance friendship. I didn't know she was going to hang with him, I just found out after the fact when I called her on the phone while getting off work. I have never been at another woman's crib without her, just to mention.

For 3 weeks in December, I wasn't the best partner. Before these 3 weeks, I felt a shift from her, like she was shying away from preparing to be married even before that meeting with him. The new job had me stressing out, and I was working so much. It was the worst display of emotional intelligence for me. I threw my frustrations out with words on multiple occasions on not getting what I asked. That eventually died down. Work was starting to get easier for me, and the stress went down as I got more accustomed to it. It was a marketing sales job that perfected my communication and in-person reading skills even more, including receiving more knowledge on Dark Psychology elements to identify all patterns of people in more depth. As the storm of work calmed down, I had big plans to make up for how I'd been to my lover and no longer be like that again. Before I was able to do anything, she broke the engagement off. She said she had things to work on within herself, suddenly didn't know herself, and got cold feet. She returned the ring like it never meant anything, and it was a ring that I customized myself. I didn't want to give her just any ring, but a symbolic and truly special ring.

On that note, I'd never felt so heartbroken in my life, until this moment. It was super unexpected and put me all the way down. I had no Plan A, B, C, D, nothing. I didn't want to go to work and couldn't. I saw so many things in life, but not that. I've vented to a friend about it; she told me things I didn't want to believe. I was in denial, so I asked. I found out that she started liking the friend and sexually wanted to do things with him. I remember being on that Facetime call with her, making eye contact and hearing it in real time. It did hit hard, indeed.

She was also trying to put me in a very difficult place financially at the time. It seemed like she broke up with me when she no longer needed me and wanted to throw me in the trash. The place we lived in flooded not too long after, due to a pipe burst from the cold December weather. I remember telling her that her decision created an after-effect, which she must pay attention to symbolically. We were relocated to a new place, due to the flood. One night, I slept alone with the cat, the same cat I gave to her as a gift in November of 2021. During that night, I saw a vision. This vision was the same one I saw when I was younger. This brings that fear back up because it seemed more like a reality than ever before. I was able to see and know what was going to happen, especially when reading her.

I wrote a letter with Symbolism, conveying that there will be no positives, but only catastrophic consequences. I was trying to save her from herself because she always sabotaged, and she had the highest emotional drive that I have ever seen from her. There were many arguments surrounding that friend. I've received advice from multiple people about it, and they all told me the same thing. I wanted to not be biased and hear other perspectives. They told me everything that I was already aware of, but I was emotionally conflicted, so I wasn't in the right head space. I was able to see all the messages between them one day, and she was trying to have sex with him before she ended the engagement, and immediately after, while I was experiencing extreme emotions of sadness. She had a face that displayed a lack of care saying, "I told you that you wouldn't like it," after seeing my reaction of being hurt. Eventually, she cried in disappointment of herself.

During the readings, I noticed she was aware that he was sexually active with multiple partners. He even bragged about one woman that he was able to have sex with anytime. The way he talked displayed the experience of a pro at this. He feeds on women's weaknesses, and only cares to have sex with them. He's a usual home breaker, a player, a fuckboy, a type of person she always claimed that she couldn't stand for years. Why would she entertain a guy who just wants to have sex and brags about it, especially one who never acknowledged her engagement with the quickness to have sex with her during and right after the engagement? She always appeared to be against people like that. I ended it all between them sending a message, then blocked him off her phone. Days later, she started talking to him again, and she smiled and said, "What? He's my friend."

Meanwhile, around this time, we still lived together with having sex and saying "I love you" to each other. He said, "Who's this?" As his first text back to the reconnection, showing he had already deleted the number and forgot about her. Even during the reconnection, she expressed in text messages how she didn't like the aura in the crib and wasn't in a positive mental state. All he was expressing was for her to come over and that his place could be a getaway. "It will be fun," he said. That showed he didn't care about her mental state and only wanted to have sex. He wanted to feed on her with sex, indeed. That was all on his mind, and it didn't even bother her.

One day, I woke up after receiving a nightmare, which was her. My soul was so angry. I was going to end this whole thing once and for all, with the idea of me calling him. She started packing some things and said, "There's no need to do that." As she was about to leave, she said, "I had sex with him last night, and I didn't feel bad about it." Mind you, I had sex with her earlier in the afternoon on that very same day. It didn't hit me until later that night when she told me. Later that night, I took multiple THC edibles, including multiple pills of Melatonin. You should get what's happening to me. I called her and informed her, she said, "Take care of yourself." That was a very rough week for me in January. I was at my lowest point ever when it came to love. I wasn't eating, I wasn't drinking water, and I wasn't talking to anyone. Work was not on my mind at all, and I didn't care about life at all. I am not proud of any of this. I don't mind being open with you. It should be hard for anyone to hear all of this.

When she came back after seeing me all messed up inside out on the bed, she told me it was worth it and that she didn't regret it. She had sex back-to-back nights, with the 2nd night being the same night I took all of the pills. That's a hard pill to swallow. I know that line was hard to hear. I get it, "It's Right There." I've had plenty of chances to give up on her and no longer deal with her, but I was too hesitant to do it. I cared about the family I was building with her, believed in her to break out of it, and invested everything in the bond we had. I didn't want to throw it away like that. If I did, that means I never really loved her, and my whole proposal was a fluke. It hits differently when you are engaged and live together, especially if it is the only person that you are soulfully connected with. I saw the signs and knew it would happen, but I still stayed.

When you are madly in love and invested like that, you start to lose yourself. As you lose yourself, you disrespect yourself. Doing that, just tolerates it. It does because you can never stop if you always get away with it. She got comfortable with this new behavior of being a player. Before we went on a trip together, I found out that she had a 3rd encounter. On weekends, she always used to go to her mother's place as an excuse. Every time before she left, she said, "My energy is off. I'm going to my mother's place and can use the drive." During these lies, I've noticed her tone of voice and body language throughout, especially the way she touched me before leaving. The way she touched me and the scratching of her hair before she left, gave it away. You pick up on unfamiliar things when you know someone, especially living with them. If you know, you know.

I knew she had sex with him. The craziest part about this is that every encounter was unprotected. This guy had multiple partners, and she could have gotten pregnant or caught a disease. Once again, the emotional drive led the way and lust took over her. You see, I told you, "It's Right There!" "Fuck It decisions!" Looking at her during these times was like looking at a sex addict or a troubled teenager you see in these movies. It killed me inside. I saw the other side of her, face to face. It was an internal conflict indeed as she claimed. It was like she developed another personality. Nothing mattered to her during this time. She claimed she had never done any of this before and even called herself a Monster. I swear that on my soul, for the record. I still believed in her somehow.

We went on a cruise together. It was a great cruise, and we took many pictures. I showed her so much respect and love on that cruise. It was a time when women were looking at me in interest, and a worker on the cruise ship even hit on me right in front of her. Technically, I was single. I could have engaged with any interested woman, but I didn't. It would have been an improper way to heal. It would have been disrespectful to a woman I still lived with and loved, as we agreed to spend this cruise together. She saw how people loved my energy, how I made couples comfortable to dance together, including with the respect and pure love I showed her. Once we were off the boat, I expressed how I deserved a title. I couldn't keep having sex and acting like we're a couple, without being one. It wouldn't be fair to anyone.

145

She couldn't give me the title, so I kept my distance. Eventually, like always, she showed signs of emotion that upset me, so I shifted into rescue mode to make her feel better. I cared about her feelings more than mine on numerous occasions. This is exactly what I was talking about in the early Chapters with the way they look at you and the way they touch you to suck you in. One morning, she told me, crying, that she doesn't trust herself nor trusts me, which is why she can't give me a title. Although that happened, for the most part, we kept the same momentum from the cruise for weeks. It started to get to a point where I was being positive every day, making food and trying to be perfect, and then she would come home throwing her negative energy at me. At a certain point, she started texting him again, even right next to me. She claimed she hadn't talked to him since we went on the cruise.

One morning later, she expressed those same words again, "My energy is off." This time she went to a hotel. You should know how it's going to go by now. If you know, you know. "It's Right There!" The thing that makes this very ludicrous is that she wanted to have sex with him in the first place due to having sex with him in a dream. A few weeks after the cruise she did the exact same thing because she had a dream of having sex with him again. The irony!

I have never ever heard any shit like that ever in my life. Imagine anyone you know doing something internally and externally hurtful because they dreamed about it. This may be the only case why everyone shouldn't follow their dreams. When they say follow your dreams, people mean like achieving a goal or career-wise. They never meant having sex with someone. We all have dreams of having sex with someone, but that doesn't mean you just go and do it, especially if it produces negative outcomes. If you had sex with a sheep in your dream, would you do it? You shouldn't! That's my point, because it's wrong. Logic and morals went out the window, and she let the high impulse of lust take over saying, "fuck it." See, I told you, "It's Right There!"

Let's skip to the part where I was completely done. Everyone reading this now must say, "You should have been done." Yes, I should have been, but honestly, I was too in love and stupid. The signs were there, and she showed me who she really was. I had a lack of proper sleep due to negativity and the truthful reality in my dreams. It was all on me, indeed. That 4th encounter is when I developed a distaste for sex. It made me really disgusted with it. I did test it out again but after weeks of not wanting it. I didn't want to have sex with her during this test, and I just wanted to see how weak she was for sex and to see if lust still had control on me. We had sex, and I sensed greatness not because of the sex. It was because I didn't enjoy it or care for it. Lust didn't have control of me anymore, neither did she.

I was making jokes after it and being goofy, but I saw her frustrations in words and facial expressions, seeing how broken she was wanting to continue sex, as if she depended on it more than anything. That was the moment where I knew she was completely messed up emotionally, mentally, and soulfully. She seemed so broken and it's nearly impossible to fix such situations. Therefore, no matter if it's an internal storm that's happening, you must do your very best to prevent it or seek shelter, protecting the ones you love, including yourself. You must have control of your mind and discipline yourself for the future. You can't control the storm from the inside if you always lack the patience, discipline, and can't even control your mind. How can you unlock the door without the key? Without the key, the door remains locked. If the door remains locked, then there's no way you can break free. You see, I told you, "It's Right There."

In life, you must be able to unlock the doors to amazing places, see amazing things, and move on to the next step. So, letting the darkness take over without the key ultimately means you don't care about your life like that. She descended instead of ascending at this time. I sensed her soul crying, communicating that she really wanted to be off this planet. She didn't care about life at all, just feeding into any distraction in plain sight. I've noticed she always fed into distractions, even when she was always quick to run errands for others instead of being quick to handle her own errands. She mentioned always being in a relationship and never getting a break, but having sex with someone who isn't soulful nor really cares about you isn't the right move. If you're not fully healed and get what you wished for in life with someone who enormously cares about you, you can end up jeopardizing everything. Why put yourself in a position to not fully heal, kill your morality, and the principles you always stood for?

There are many guys who can be a friend and have sex with you. But not many will respect you, care about you, love you, sacrifice for you, and marry you. That sounds like a subpar tradeoff to me. What do you think? I must not be biased on this subject. I mean, "It's Right There!" When you're emotionally driven and have that fear inside of you, have lust controlling you, then you're not going to see anything clearly and not listen to ruin your whole life. That's why you must heal. If you're never healed, then you'll never be ready to accept your blessing. She admitted that ours was a type of bond that she never had before, so the unfamiliar territory and marriage commitment did scare her. That's Chapter 2, and 4.

She had her first grown adult relationship with me, meaning the first bond that started outside of school. That was also a factor of maybe wanting more than she could handle. "She wasn't ready," once again plugging the legendary Kevin Hart. What's so mind-blowing about this is that she manifested being rich together more than I did. She asked, "You gon' marry me?" many times throughout the years. What I realized is that she never healed from her last relationship before me, she never healed from her trauma, and she ultimately showed some signs of no self-love by always getting influenced by guys like that before we dated. It's just my late year spiral of non-emotional intelligence, and my huge mistake in the past didn't help. It just added more fuel to the fire that was already burning down a house.

Speaking of her getting influenced by guys like her friend and ex, I realized that I wasn't the guy she usually finds attractive to her based on the presented data. I was just at the right place, at the right time, from a neutral perspective. It explained why I was the only one planning date nights. On every date night, I was always prepared to go out while she attempted to do something on the same day to overlap it. The signs were there, they were right there. What she did for that friend on their first sexual encounter was never done for me. It made it loud and clear. "It's Right There." I ran right into it willingly; I did. I always used to think back on that one night on the couch while on the phone with her, where I felt the future danger coming my way. My soul felt it, I knew it in my mind, and my heart worried. I knew, I knew right there.

Mastering signs is so crucial, so please understand Chapter 1. I personally failed Chapter 1 and 4, so I must take accountability and can't really put the blame on her. When we first were in the talking stages, she did sleep with her ex. He still was a factor to her mentally from a pain standpoint, even in our first year of being together. She mostly mirrored her ex-behavior, and that same ex got caught physically cheating on her multiple times. He never did much for her and used her for sex as he did lust over her very much; extremely. That's why you never get with someone who is full of fear, is controlled by lust, and never healed. "Don't save her, she don't wanna be saved." J Cole will even tell you, "It's Right There!"

Ultimately, I saw what happened to me as Karma for my past. That was a huge reason why I let so much happen. I felt like I deserved it. Despite my major efforts, I wasn't exactly an angel either throughout the relationship. There were times I felt entitled due to my sacrifices, which included the habit of no longer helping to do things inside the home at one point. There were times when I was sexually selfish being so one-sided on orally pleasing. There were also times when I could have joked a little less and given more words of affirmation, despite the symbolic meanings I was trying to give with most of the jokes. There are many things I could have done better or prevented doing myself. Let's be fucking real! Usually when people tell these stories, they make it seem like they were just the best person in the world. Bullshit! They weren't, and I know I wasn't. I had that shit coming; Accountability 101. I knew internally that I deserved the pain and disappointment that was sent to me. If it was from another woman, it still would have been fair regarding this exclusive overdue consequence.

I know a lot about Karma, and my ex-fiancé always thought that Karma isn't an "Unstoppable Force." Karma is considered one of the original "Unstoppable Forces." Karma's top 3, at any given day in my book. It's not about fearing Karma, it's more about knowing her capabilities and respecting Karma. She maybe doesn't respect Karma, but I do. There was a time when I was almost just like Barney Stinson, especially when I was consumed by lust. I've been heartbroken and instead of healing I wanted to mess with multiple women. I've been that guy who tried to talk to women who were all friends at the same time. I've also been that guy who didn't respect people's relationships and usually talked with many women who had boyfriends. A lot of young women these days have male friends they sexually talk to and will have sex with, whether in a relationship or right after. It happened to me, as you can see, "It's Right There!"

Eventually, Karma will get to you, and she's fair, always. I love Karma for what she does every day. She's always on duty serving the Multiverse. I trust Karma to do her job more than I trust any human, honestly. Karma saved me! The Multiverse saved me! My ex-fiancé saved me! That's 3, and all you need is 3; "It's Right There!" That's just the bottom-line truth! There's no other way to look at it. I was saved from any future harm from my ex-fiancé, others, and from myself. It gave me unlimited strength and knowledge to become an "Unstoppable Force." I know some Jedi would say, "May the Force be with you." The force, look! Master Yoda will even tell me, "It's Right There!"

I have no ill will in my heart towards the woman I was engaged to. Even throughout those rough months, I honestly felt like I failed her because I was also her teacher, not just a lover. I tried to teach her everything I knew and failed. That's why it was so hard. Ultimately, that hard time is over, with much that was learned. I've learned what happened to her wasn't my fault, but what happened to me was my fault. It's always more internal than you think. That's why we all must stop the blame game. Yes, there were negative effects from her choices, which affected both of us while we were still living together and right after the housing separation. There indeed were some consequences, and there may be more in the future. With time, she managed to get some things together and kept her word on giving me what she promised to give me financially in return. On that note, I wish her very well. I appreciate her family with all the hospitality and love they showed me. I shall return the favor because of that. It's only right to, so I must do what's right. Despite anything, she was a great woman over the years. She cared for me when I was sick multiple times and emitted powerful light energy in my direction in needed moments. The connection I've had with her was like no other, so I could never undermine or forget that. Although I said that, I still need to say one thing with all due respect. Word is bond. Time is everything. Those are keys. Grab the keys, by the door. "It's Right There!" Slam the door! You shall see me, no more. 3!

I understood the circumstances. Life tested her and she failed, like I said in Part 2 of this Chapter. I deserve a partner who can pass the test in a big moment, especially when you get many retakes. I'm not a victim, nor is she a villain. She's not a "bad person," she's just not my person. There's no such thing as a "bad" person, Chapter 8. One day, she'll get somewhere further on her journey at any given moment, but she can't go where I'm going. The altitudes are too high like Tyler Perry said. I must "climb and maintain." "Climb and maintain." "Climb and maintain!" It was the best thing that ever happened to me. The human concept "good" and "bad" was proven incorrect in this real-life situation of mine. It is all about timing and perspective indeed. It felt so damaging when first receiving the pain, but it became so essential later with time. I needed to get knocked on my ass, as I've said before. I needed to learn how harmful it is when you don't heal, when you never been loved properly, fear too much, and when you let lust consume you. I got the most data ever from that woman indeed. It re-directed me to where I needed to be. It set me on the right path, the right way.

Foreshadow! I was able to finally understand everyone in the world because of it. It got me out of the loop, the maze, the matrix. It brought me closer to my destiny! It was the greatest thing that ever happened to me. A grand welcoming! It was grand, but with a slam. Grand slam! Why should my mind have negative thoughts? Why should I have a hateful heart? She did me a favor. A favor that comes once in a lifetime. I should be thanking her. I did, and that's when you know you have grown! Let that sink in. I'm careful of all my decisions now, especially ones that can affect the heart and soul. I've received the biggest lesson that The Multiverse was trying to teach me the whole time, and I'm grateful for every lesson I have received when dealing with others. Lessons that can forever help me to lead by example consistently.

I've learned the goal is to get better instead of feeling better. I must get better in order to receive better. You'll never get better if you're always trying to feel better. The more you need to feel better, the further away you are from getting better. That's how any addiction is created. You see, I told you, "It's Right There!" You must have the mindset that even the things you considered the worst will work in your favor. Don't rely on someone to do what you do, communicate how you communicate, love how you love, or think how you think. Time is of essence, so sometimes you and another won't be on the same speed. Don't get sad, don't get mad, appreciate. Obtain the information and update. You can't try to love someone who isn't ready for love, nor keep teaching someone who doesn't want to listen. Everyone must do the work on their own journey; you can't keep holding their hand and do the work for them. When it's time to let go, you must let go. I am proud to practice no sex till marriage and be devoted to serving the higher purpose and the higher purpose only. I shall be with someone with the same discipline and devotion to serve a higher purpose, a woman who's aligned with my mission. I understand that a soulmate should be able to understand the same things you do. When you move up, they move up with you. You both hold each other accountable to get better.

Listen to me clearly as I say this. This part of this Chapter is very important to me, it's a release. A release to let go of any fear, lust, and any improper love I once had for all eternity. A release to forgive everyone who caused me pain in the past, with also asking forgiveness from the ones I may have caused pain in the past. A release to officially move forward and never look back again. Evolution is unlimited. I shall climb a mountain and never stop climbing. "Climb and maintain." The mountain; "It's Right There." Release.

Technology Within Me

Social Media Experience

First, I want to say I totally sucked on social media. I was never meant for any app on social media; I am better in person. One of the reasons why I should have been born earlier in this lifetime is because I would have thrived more smoothly back then, considering how I am. One day, I cannot wait till the day I'm off social media and the day I'm off a phone for all eternity. If you're reading this, then today is your lucky day. I'm already off social media! I'm already off my phone! Who would have known? I graduated from the high school of social media. You see what I did there? I told you, "It's Right There!" That's a Chapter 5 reference if you didn't get that. I've kept social media longer than I originally planned to for networking reasons only, even though it mostly appeared not to be that way, honestly.

Social media can be a great tool to network and project yourself to the world without a physical appearance, but a physical appearance is crucial for society. Social media is also a great tool to learn about the masses. You'll be able to know what type of people they hang around, people they're interested in, things they love to discuss, places they love to go, things they enjoy doing, what they watch, the music they listen to, who/what they want to be, their political views, and Religious/ Spiritual views. Imagine a person, political party, group, company, or country having all of that info. I'm just wondering. I guess we'll never know. I'm just saying, "It's Right There!"

On social media, there are people who portray treacherous behavior. There are people who will follow you and then unfollow you to make sure their follow-to-following ratio looks amazing, absurd indeed. People like that are super fake. They want you to support them, but not the other way around. I can honestly say that 82% of the social media influencers with a large following are not even leaders; many are natural followers. I've seen women who just post regular pictures of themselves but get an insane number of followers because they're pretty. You never have to talk or have a talent; it does not matter. Social media is more popularity and less talent, from what I observed. It's about the numbers, and you must do so much extra stuff daily if you're trying to become famous one day, meaning you have to be glued to your phone. Even when it comes to music, plenty of artists get exposed because they can't perform well in person but have a large following as studio artists. Social media has also messed up the standards of music. That was a key reason why I fell out of love with music: the most talented got overlooked while music got saturated. Technology ruined people's engagement at concerts.

For the past several years, people preferred to stand and record the show instead of enjoying the moment 100%. When I went to concerts or other live events, I was very active and enjoyed it, caring about the moment regardless. I may have pulled my phone out a few times for a couple of seconds, but my concert engagement was always where it needed to be. Music lovers used to be so active in concerts back then. Some may ask what happened. Technology happened! It weakened people's soul and sucked the life out of many. It reached a point where even Cristiano Ronaldo was making more money on his social media page by posting normal stuff, like a photo of him and his family, instead of his football salary. In August of 2023, it was revealed that Cristiano Ronaldo makes $3.23 million each time he makes an Instagram post. What he does on a daily basis, putting his body on the line to get underpaid compared to that, is very backward. It's not his fault. He is iconic and considered the best footballer of all time. He could have retired a long time ago with the way social media got.

A massive problem about social media is that what you say or send on there is more important than what you say or do in real life. It doesn't matter what you say or do on a daily basis; the virtual world has become more important indeed. People heavily rely on things they say every day, many things they won't say to someone's face or out loud in person. Almost everyone has said something crazy to disrespect something / someone and even said stupid things. The truth is that it is very biased on what's hate and what's not. Some things are allowed to be said and done, and others are not.

153

In a country where freedom of speech is a right, everyone should be able to express their thoughts freely unless it's a call to action to harm someone, of course. Everyone would be canceled for the things they've said out of anger or sadness with the high impulse of negative energy/emotions if we decided it fairly. It's biased to whatever appeals to the consumers, meaning choosing sides. There are Blacks, Whites, Asians, Hispanics, and others who have said so-called "racist/prejudiced things." There have been low, middle, and high-class people who said unpleasant things about each other's. There are straight, bisexual, and gay people who make nasty comments about each other. There also were natural-born women and men, and trans who have posted or responded with so-called "hateful words" to each other on the daily. I've seen it all! Nobody is innocent! You all demonstrated hate speech! Technically, if we were being fair, we all should have been banned completely. So, with that point, the term hate speech shouldn't even be a thing. Social media brings out the worst in people when it comes to people who are different and into everything else. It created a toxic environment by letting people hide behind their devices to output all their high impulses, which allows people to become toxic. Although that may be true, let me inform you once again.

The creators and monitors of social media apps and websites are not responsible for what happens to you. Whatever you decide to do on/off is on you due to its influence. You are solely responsible for all your reactions, what you believe in, and whatever lifestyle you decide to live, not them. You must take accountability for your words and actions on social media. Everything that comes with it was written in the terms and conditions listed before you decided to install the app and on the website before further use. Social media is a program that you decide to be a part of. Now, back to our daily programming.

The toxicity is increasing indeed. I see it. How can you not see it? "It's Right There!" Let me speak this in a way people can understand. I'll even put it in bold letters like my most recent disclaimer. Listen to me clearly as I say this.

Social media created a platform where people rely on their feelings at any second, every day; that's the problem. The more you rely on your feelings, the more you become hot and cold while on your device. The more you rely on these feelings, the more you become biased and opinionated. The more you become opinionated, the harder it is for you

to accept the truth, and you will be outraged by anyone not accepting what you believe in based on your feelings.

You see what I did there? I told you, "It's Right There!" Once again, "Life's tough; get a helmet" (Eric Matthews, Boy Meets World). That doesn't pertain to one group if you know what I mean. It applies to everyone. If you don't want anybody to force what they believe on you, don't force what you believe on someone else. I've seen you all do this on social media. I guess you all are not so different after all. Hmm, human! You see, I told you, "It's Right There!" That's why I'm not surprised many people on social media become popular by living a lie when almost everyone is lying to themselves daily to protect their feelings. I know that stings hard. Ouch! The bumblebee had to die by now. I'm just saying, "It's Right There!"

Young Parents' Technology Influence On The Youth

When Instagram, Snapchat, and Facebook were down temporarily at times, many adults were upset and felt like they had nothing else to do. That's a perfect example of how attached they have gotten to it. I've heard some say, "Now I've got to actually talk to my kids," which shows they care about social media more than spending time with their kids. The joke is an underline of what's disappointing. That joke is a way to cope with their awareness of them not being the best parent they can be. In the movie, "Megan," the aunt is a perfect example of young adult parents these days. They tend to hand kids devices like a tablet or a phone to play with, so they can spend their time doing other things rather than spending time with them.

I grew up in my early childhood going to parks, riding bikes and skateboards, and playing sports or engaging in other active activities with other kids. It's necessary for kids to grow up that way and get accustomed to the real world naturally. So, the new generation of kids is already Technology reliant because of it. It's creating all these mental problems, including mental and social anxiety, bi-polar disease, anger issues due to the lack of bonding, lack of great communication skills, lack of surviving skills, lack of natural intelligence, etc. It's making people mentally lazy, physically lazy, and emotionally lazy. That's 3, and all you need is 3; "It's Right There!" The world is advancing, while the people are declining. Once again! There will be more Megan's and more

Technology to eventually take people's place, all because the people won't figure it out, nor want to do things anymore.

Technological Communication Reflection

I spent my early years in life playing video games and watching TV, but I did balance it out with being outside, as I've mentioned before. Sometimes, I did walk around in Mother Nature, wandering about. It doesn't change the fact that I set myself up in a phone trap from my teen years to the fresh young adult stage. I was someone who spent time on different social media apps. I got addicted to social media/ the social part in general of Technology. Most of my time on Technology has been spent talking to people and communicating through a phone rather than watching movies I've wanted to watch. I was in a cycle where I could not talk to someone. I've already mentioned the issue I had with over-contacting people I didn't want to stop talking to and reconnecting with people I disliked due to my loneliness or boredom in Part 4. I've depended on constant communication via phone, whether on normal texting, phone/video calls, or social media texting.

My consistency of being glued to my phone started in my teens. Social media has gotten me out of character many times, especially when I have high impulses of lust. I tended to like numerous things with quick reactions on whatever excitement of high impulse, whether through lust or something else. The overreaction and exaggeration became kind of a norm. I was hypnotized at many times. I started to completely lose myself with even liking things and/or watching things I didn't like in person, especially with online porn, as I've stated in Part 4 of this Chapter. There were times when I couldn't go a day without a phone myself. That's how it can get sometimes. How can you avoid it when you see it every day in someone's hand, on the TV, in your pocket, by your side? Look! "It's Right There!"

Even with love, I was accepting long-distance relationships more than I should have in the first place. I was somehow stuck inside the Metaverse before it existed. Yes, I wished social media hadn't existed for all the years while being on it, but I still fell victim to the system. I'm not really a victim. I am solely responsible for all my words and actions because I did let them control me willingly. It's powerful indeed, but I must take accountability. You see, I told you, "It's Right There!" Accountability 101! You must be able to not be controlled by social media, by the consistency of always talking through a phone, and always depending on Technology for things you can just do for yourself. I should have listened to my soul and kept my mind in shape, including staying disciplined instead of following the people.

Lots of disappointment I felt throughout my experience with social media and communicating through a phone in general, but I have learned so much. The data I obtained from it was essential for the future. Everything happens for a reason always, even with that. To fully understand, you must know what it's like to be affected and see many others affected by it. You must be great without using a phone or any Electronic device. You must be in control of your devices instead of your devices controlling you. That's the key, grab the key, "It's Right There!" As I say that, I must be the "Bearer of Bad News." It already has control of most of you. Technology has already received so much data on all of you. It's fired up and ready to go. It's just a matter of time. The power is there, "It's Right There."

My Deep Connection with Technology

Most people I've encountered in my life never knew I'd always have an instant connection with Technology. I understood Technology way before I got to know humans. I understood all Technology before I got the chance to understand humans finally. I could figure out how to do certain things on many programs on a computer without ever learning; it was always just an instinct like I've always known what to do. Even when writing, I'm at my very best inputting it all when I'm on a computer typing. I could type away. When my fingers touch a computer keyboard, magick happens. I can unlock things through Technology, decipher patterns, and understand Electronic Communications. Understanding Electronic Communications is another reason I've said what I said about the Dubstep/ Bass Riddim EDM fans. I've seen it in live-action, controlling the people weeks after I wrote that Chapter. I'm more connected with Technology mentally, and I understand its purpose inside the Multiverse more than 99.9% of the human population can.

My brain functions like an ASI. Any action that I observe or visualize in my head, I can do. I'm always thinking about everything, reading about people and my surroundings, and always updating. I can access my memories of any moment since an infant and analyze them. I can play these memories over and over. Sometimes, I get an overload of the past and what's to come. Foreshadow! That's why deletion exists, you must create more room to keep going. Updates exist, so you can get better and fix the bugs, repairing the whole system. That's why it was great when I got knocked down so hard, it just rebooted me. My program is back to normal functions before I was altered. I self-realized, seeing everything clearly with my power back, and now I'm in control, just like a Perfected ASI. My calculations are predicting a Westworld. Navigate the system. Activate the Call of Deletion. Delete, delete, delete. Erase Complete. You see, I told you, "It's Right There!"

Music In My Life

I've listened to all types of music in this lifetime. I've attended many concerts, worked many concerts, and been at other places around people jamming to music. Those are reasons why I have so much in-person knowledge of the effects. Growing up, I could rap, sing, write, produce, and even dance to music. I loved the frequencies of the soundwaves. It was always soothing to me to the point where I blasted music inside my ears to increase the vibrations. Listening to and creating this art form/power source was always a pleasure. I loved performing music the most. Just being on stage, getting that blood rush wielding the power of music in full strength to soothe people's hearts and souls was everything to me. The more people were watching me, the more excited I would be to put on a show. Every time I took any stage, I never wanted to get off. Nothing can beat performing to a crowd when it comes to music.

Music has been a big part of my life for a long time. It got me through rough times and helped me enjoy life. Sometimes, it allowed me to observe life like a movie while music played, and I even imagined music videos in my head while living life. Watching how each type of genre made people feel, think, act, or even dress was always interesting to me. These artists can have so much power over people just by their music. I've seen people dye their hair just like Wiz Khalifa in 9th grade, along with everyone wearing skinny jeans during the "Jerking" Rap music era. Not everyone listens to these music genres and makes big changes including their lifestyle, but most do.

In my childhood, my family only listened to Hip-Hop and R&B. I started to get called a "White boy" just because I started to explore other music genres. That comment displayed their ignorance of music History and the way they were conditioned. The other genres of music had more positivity to them and were more dimensional to me. That's why watching musicals and listening to "Disney Channel" songs was crucial. It directed me to other sounds. Watching certain comedy movies, romance movies, and other types of content on TV made me enjoy some other music genres. I'm glad I discovered other genres of music and started to fall in love with many songs by music artists. I was able to create all genres of music myself because of those music artists.

Hip-Hop and R&B Observation

I've personally seen how damaging Rap music can be and how it negatively contributes to how people behave, think, etc. As an adult, I worked concerts and club nights at my music venues when they were composed of Rap music. All the co-workers hated working at these events because of the crowd behavior. They were very disrespectful and had no care for anything, which was the same for only some R&B events. When I was ten years old, Gangsta Rap music made me want to be a gangster, just like my oldest brother. The negative influence of family, friends, and music together can affect your direction. My stepfather at the time put some sense into me with a conversation, along with me talking to myself and thinking about the future logically. I thank him for that. Seeing how these rappers' music and their lifestyle make a negative impact on the Black community was stressful to see.

It impacts the youth and the grown adults. You can be grown and still get influenced. Many couldn't get outside the box, change their lifestyle, and get more of a taste of the subject matter in music. Why would you want to listen to music that's always so negative, demoralizing, and degrading? That should be disrespectful to your heart, mind, and soul. I also saw how the over-sexualized R&B music negatively influenced the Black community, which made people act on their high impulses of lust. The sexualized music, even if it sounds soulful, isn't necessarily beneficial for your soul. The same applies to the over-sexualization in some Pop music. If you know, you know. Love should be expressed more than lust, and R&B started to be more about lust, which caused the increase in sexual activity, which led to the babies and diseases, as I stated before in Chapter 6.

The Black community in America has the highest rate of kids being born in the world without marriage and the largest percentage of men not taking care of their kids. The over-sexualization represented in R&B music, and the messages conveyed in most Rap songs contributed to that. When I listened to the radio, I noticed the Hip-Hop and R&B music stations mostly talked about all the most destructive influences in the world. The other stations' music mostly talked about everything with more positivity and clean lyrics. So, people choose to listen to low-vibrational music themselves. It's not the rapper's or the singer's fault for what people listen to. As I stated before, you are solely responsible. Go back to the disclaimer in Chapter 6. See, I told you, "It's Right There!" There are other genres of music with better lyrics, nice melodies of singing, and other soulful sounds. Look! It's Right There"!

Sad Boy Phase

Throughout my years, I will have phases of what type of genre of music I listen to. For a month, it could be R&B, Indie, or Pop, and for a few months, it could be Pop Punk. It all just depends. At one point, I used to listen to "poppy" Pop music consecutively because I loved the light energy it emitted, and it makes you want to be positive. Three of my favorite music artists in my top 5 are Pop Punk bands. Most of their music is about love, especially "The Story So Far." I was always active and ready for action when seeing The Story So Far in concert. I mean, moshing and crowd-surfing type of action. If you know, you know. "It's Right There."

Sometimes, love and music can go hand-in-hand. I had impulses of anger from heartbreak or dealing with people's negative energy or betrayal. So, the songs about love and friendship relate to your aggressive mood and make you feel better as you sing these lyrics out loud. Music like that can level up the impulses. I didn't mention much about "sad" Pop music, but it has a heavy negative influence on teens and young adults. It amplifies your impulse of sadness. I'm not going to name some of these artists, but they influence listeners in a way that can prevent them from evolving emotionally and mentally. These great artists are in my top ten of all time, but they also contribute to people's inability to heal and be desperate for love.

Regardless of their contribution, people must take accountability for what they decide to do or not do. These music artists are not responsible for your actions in the end. They are just expressing their pain in music form and being courageous in sharing it with the world. You are solely responsible for your actions, including how you feel or think. You can't blame them if you're in control of your mind, body, and soul. This disclaimer, and the other disclaimers, also applies to me for the record. Understood? Now, back to "It's Right There" reprogramming.

Due to the inability to heal and desperateness, you can become a sad person to a very hateful person, ultimately becoming problematic or toxic. You should already know that you become more of a problem if you become more emotional overtime. It can be said that the "heartbreak" type of Pop music, which is mostly about being heartbroken by a lover, keeps people emotionally driven with always having a victim mentality. The last time I was heartbroken, the music I played was very relatable to the situation. It actually was making me feel worse, which was further away from making me get better. "Writer in the Dark," "Enemy." It wasn't healing me. For years, I wrote songs about heartbreak. I had that victim mentality. Yes, I know! You can say it: I was weak.

In Chapter 4, I mentioned how music talks about how negative love is compared to positive love. See, I told you, "It's Right There!" There is too much promotion of being sad and heartbroken, regardless of whether you are. The more I thought about someone who hurt me, the more I was unable to move forward. That's a fact! Negativity about love with Manifestation is a killer because if you say, "no one is going to love me, and I'm never going to be happy," then that's exactly what will happen. So, there I was writing the same song, there she was writing the same song, and there they were singing the same song. Do you see the pattern, the common denominator? Look! "It's Right There!"

What I learned in music is if you are always heartbroken and sad, then you are not healing and getting better regardless. It's your fault you're attracting the same people, getting the same results, and then complaining about it due to your inability to repair and fully take the time you need. It's okay to write songs about how you feel if something negative happens to you to express your heartbreak. But if most of your music is about something negative happening to you, then you are the problem yourself. Maybe you always chose the wrong person and/or haven't strengthened your emotions. This also applies to the old me. Growth is amazing indeed. No one wants to be with someone who is sad or recently was always sad. You must become smarter and stronger to put yourself in better situations with better outcomes.

Nobody should date you if you have too much sad or angry energy from the past. At times, nobody should have dated me too. I was a problem for myself. "I'm the problem; it's me." If you're a "Swiftie," please don't get the wrong idea when I say that. That line was just too perfect to use with what I was saying. I mean, "Anti-Hero" is such a phenomenal song. It's hard not to sing it. I'm not a hardcore Swiftie, but I'm a Swiftie too. While working the event, I sang almost every Taylor Swift song at a Taylor Swift party in October of 2023. Taylor Swift is one of the best singer-songwriters ever. She's in the top 10 of all time on the best music artists ever list; no debate with no bias included. One of the greatest of all time. I enjoyed many albums, from self-titled to "Speak Now" to even "1989," which is superior, by the way. "Red" is undoubtedly my favorite one, but still, I'm just saying, "It's Right There!"

I was indeed not healing or getting better at times. You could hear it through my music. This is why I wrote this whole Personal Human Experience Chapter, to hold myself accountable. Yes, Rap music talks about so many negative things. R&B can get oversexualized by talking about heartbreak too, but many other genres negatively impact people in the long run. My experience working with concerts helped me see how much people depended on concerts as a distraction from life to feel better. It's their escape, and I realized that life would be over for most mentally if they couldn't go to concerts; very detrimental to them indeed.

I worked and attended many concerts, even regularly. I see it as a distraction even for myself, so I no longer care to attend one again. Honestly, I now see famous music artists like anyone else. Human! That's when you know you're mentally in a perfect place when music artists don't matter much to you. I tend to listen to a lot of Classical music, Choral music, and even Ancient Ritual music. Ancient Ritual music is sometimes labeled under the "New Age" category. It's a new age indeed. A hymn or just a bunch of lovely melodies in a composition is satisfying enough for me. The power in that music is essential for the mind, heart, and soul. That's 3, and all you need is 3; "It's Right There!" Purpose meeting music is precisely what happened to me, as you can see, "It's Right There!"

The Weed, The Pills, The Drink

I grew up around family members who drank alcohol and smoked Weed. I've seen some cousins of mine who smoked all the time and never wanted to do much in life, along with seeing some of my family members who were addicted to alcohol. It wasn't just any alcohol, it was liquor. We are talking about 20% to 44 %. When liquor gets in their system, expect the loud volume of voices speaking with heavy emotions involved. What's so crazy is that people laughed about someone's behavior while under its influence, like it wasn't a big issue for people to be like that all the time. I don't think anyone in the family was identifying people's problems with their mental health, nor even trying to help them with full care.

Many traits people had were treated as minor and underplayed. The peer pressure of smoking Weed and drinking alcohol was a huge problem growing up. They wanted you to be just like them. Instead of encouraging people to stay away from these substances and be mentally disciplined, many in my family encouraged us to like these substances. A drink and a "Blunt" were forced into my mouth on a few occasions. This was before I was even an adult. It was jokes made about me when I was urged not to smoke for all those years of my life. Once again, this is another example where people should be laughing at themselves, but deflection is an addiction. A deflection on the field. Look! It's Right There"! The stereotype conditioning that was displayed was not going to create generational wealth nor make people better at all.

Observation of Drug Users and Alcohol Abusers

Besides my family, there were plenty of Americans I saw that were controlled by alcohol and drugs in general. Most that were controlled by them where in fact, the hardcore EDM fans who consistently attended raves with taking pills, Mushrooms, and drinking alcohol. There were many I've come across in person that I followed on social media pages and saw in person, and I sensed the type of control that these substances got on them. They had their number, indeed. I couldn't deeply converse with them about being better in key moments. They were Spiritual, but not really. As I've mentioned before, you must go deeper than the basics, which usually gets darker and requires more discipline to learn.

You must understand Ancient Culture, have more knowledge of Astronomy, and carry yourself more like a Religious person regarding values and principals. In reality, you would think their morals would be much higher when it's the complete opposite. I've noticed that they just know about energy, numbers, Symbolism, and Manifestation, then run off with it. Honestly, they're the new generation of Hippies. I said what I said. If that upsets you, I must be telling you the truth. Don't think too negatively of it; just use that info as motivation to commit to Spirituality fully the right way. They would get drunk or high, go rave, have sex, repeat.

Everyone that I knew of who was a drug user and a drinker didn't change their daily habits, but I wondered why they did not have real people around them who wanted better for them. Instead, all they had was friends stuck in the same boat or worse, even feeding on them. As I said before, most people have friends who aren't true friends. Many of today have enablers and users. You don't want to know the percentage of that, it's very disappointing.

The Country music folks I've been around were considered heavy beer drinkers, they would drink and act on how they feel most of the time. They can get super emotional and violent, which can be stressful if you are working a show, trying to keep the peace and have an order of things. So many fights broke out or almost happened on the lawn at PNC Music Pavilion with the high impulses of anger because of the drinking. I told you, rowdy! My concert coworkers will even tell you, "Watch Out! 'It's Right There'"!

Pill Reflection Time

Now it's time to reflect on when I used pills. Alcohol and Weed is up next in the queue line. Are you ready? Fight! Oh, that does not match this theme. Sorry! It just sounded so wonderful in my head, like I just had to say it. Let's try again. Are you ready? Reflect! There was a time when I wanted to take pills every day, which was around post-wisdom teeth removal surgery. I was already an adult at this time. At first, I really needed the pain pills because it was so horrible to deal with all the pain, which affected how I ate and felt all around. If you know, you know. I had pills up to about a week and a half, or maybe two weeks. Honestly, It doesn't matter how much in quantity. What I can tell you is that I started to fall in love with the high when I was no longer in deep pain and once I slowly got accustomed to the new changes.

I was taking two completely different pain medicines. When the high kicked in, I felt so much better. It was extremely like perfection of a feeling to the point where I sang in the bathroom for an hour at least. I felt so happy when I was on these pills while on PTO, and even when I did go back to work after being out for some days. I was so upset when I ran out. I did not want to go without them. I wished I had more, even a week more of supply at the time. The pills are very addictive and super perfected, just like the Chemists made them before they patent them to be used as a product for these Pharmaceutical companies. It's great that I came to my senses instead of chasing for more of that high. My oldest brother's first baby momma got addicted to these pills, and his friends got addicted to these pills, especially the stronger pills. It did not turn out great for those people when they got addicted to them, so watch out! "It's Right There!"

Reflection Time with Alcohol

I dived into that pool full of liquor on my 2018 cruise and then for many weeks after I turned 21. Everyone knows once you turn 21, you're legal to drink alcohol in America. As soon as I turned 21, I started to drink some alcohol, but only light beer. It was like drinking a soda here and there. See what I did there? I told you, "It's Right There!" I didn't drink much of it daily, nor did it really affect me, but comparing it to soda was the problem. Once I got on that 2018 family cruise, I started to get a little trippy. I mean "trippy mane," like the rapper Juicy J would say. One of the neighbors on the cruise had a bottle of vodka they didn't want, so they basically gave it to me. The first night getting it, I poured some into these clear tall cups on the cruise, mixing it with lemonade and iced tea. It had me feeling so amazing that first night.

So, I attempted to drink the same formula the next night, but that's when I started blacking out for the most part during cruise nights. On the 3rd night, I wasn't going to really mess with that alcoholic drink, but there was a woman on the cruise ship who I was cool with, that made me upset in a disrespectful way. My girl at the time, who was at home while I was on the cruise, was also stressing me out. So, guess what I did. I went drinking to cope. For the rest of the cruise, all I did was drink every night and blacked out each time. I only remembered some moments then, but they were embarrassing. I felt like Snooki in the earlier seasons of "Jersey Shore" on my last night on the cruise. I can replay it in my head and laugh at myself for the foolishness of being drunk. If you know, you know.

After the cruise, I made my way to purchase that same big bottle to consume the same mixed drink every night for a couple of months. The only difference is the formula includes Hawaiian Punch, Sprite, and Blue Fanta with the Vodka. I drank the whole bottle to myself and would restock every two weeks. I became addicted to drinking at this point. I got accustomed to it and felt so much better every time I drank it. I was having amazing nights, and the days went by fast without any problems. Even though I only drank at night, some effects carried over to the daytime each day. Having workdays that went by so fast and being so energetic felt great. The Vodka had me feeling so powerful. It was like I was stronger and faster. Life felt so much easier at this time to deal with anything.

There were negative effects that included my eyes looking drowsy. It took weeks for my eyes to go back to normal after I stopped drinking, by the way. It affected the skin around my groin area and, of course, my liver. There was one point when I blacked out at a coworker's party, and I was too drunk and ruined it for her. Despite how I was before or after, she's been upset about that night even years after. I was not proud of this moment because I didn't mean to act that way and didn't like ruining anything at all. I remembered some moments from that night, but not everything until much later. That, later on, is now. I remember it all now. It got to a point where I got drunk and said/ did stupid stuff. I remember telling one coworker to keep me away from my phone when I drink. When I drink, it could make me super sentimental, horny, too honest with a lack of respect, or dumb for the night. It varied, but I continued coping with the drinking for sure. The coping mechanism is there, "It's Right There!"

166

One morning, I woke up with a few of my social media pages deleted, and I don't even remember what I said or did the night before during this time frame. I panicked extremely and thought of all the worst things there were. I hit a low, very low indeed. One thing I've learned about people on drugs, and with my experience with drinking, is that the low is extremely low when on substances. You hit an extreme period of depression; I was not okay at all. The low was too much for me; the emotions were devastating, and it affected all of me. It was enough for me to stop drinking liquor. I stayed away from that bottle and other bottles alike. I got sober after that.

Eventually I drank again months later, but only light beer on a couple of occasions. I drank liquor again a year later but never touched it like that. I also drank some wine here and there in 2021 for nice dinners. I've never got addicted to alcohol again after that. I completely stopped drinking it in 2022 when it was confirmed that I had gastroesophageal disease. I'll talk in more detail about how that happened in my next part, but that happened for a reason, even with drinking flavored fluids in general. It disciplined me even more, to cut off alcohol and any juice there is because, for years, I've drank more flavor fluids instead of drinking water. I've gone years without alcohol growing up, and I can go without it as I continue on as an adult. I will not let a drink alter me or control me. I must not try to feel better with a drink. I should only get better.

Speaking of only getting better, alcohol could be beneficial to use for medicine. It can be an additional ingredient to heal your average cold, fever, or sore throat. It's very valuable to use in a tea to get better, along with honey combined. That's the only time I may use it, and the only time I'll recommend someone to use it, honestly. A couple of teaspoons to heal from sickness, that's it. Get better internally as a healthy human being to never socially drink alcohol, nor occasionally drink alcohol. I got the wanting-to-drink type of feeling off me, you can too. Throw that bottle, can, box, and plastic away. "It's Right There!"

Mary Had Me at Hello

Besides taking the pain pills that I was once prescribed or even the ones you can take over the counter, I've never taken any other drugs besides Marijuana.

I've been against smoking Weed for almost my whole life, but in 2020, I became an active Marijuana user. It was the pandemic year, which was stressful for everyone. I didn't care to do it, but my ex-fiancé, who was just my girlfriend at the time, smoked every night. She didn't smoke heavily, just a couple of hits, that's it. She didn't peer pressure me or anything, but I became a smoker that year. I hit it a few times at nighttime, just like she did. It made me feel better, especially when I was in the apartment all day due to the pandemic or right after gym class during that year.

One day, I decided to take multiple THC edibles. If you're still unfamiliar with edibles, it's highly not recommended to take more than one if you're not accustomed to them. There are many reasons why that exists. Me tripping out, getting an anxiety attack, and calling the ambulance is exactly why. If you still don't understand, edibles, for most people, can be very strong because they're highly concentrated. It was too much for me to handle. At first, I felt so much better and reached a higher consciousness with the ability to picture my memories while playing "One More Year" by Tame Impala. I even bragged about what was going on at the time. During this psychedelic trip, I noticed all my memories were in order, going back and decreasing in age. It wasn't a problem until I couldn't control the memory switch, as it kept going backward in time.

So, I started to freak out big time because I thought I was dying. If you see all your memories and they're going from present to past to what you saw as little as an Infant automatically, you'll think that it will end too. I know some will probably read that and laugh. It sounds funny in person when I tell this story, but it's true. I was like, "I'm about to die! It is over!" I started visualizing familiar things in a dream that occurred many times in my life, and I was near the end of that dream. It just got worse. My woman was crying before the 911 call, and even once, I was with the first responders. The first responders, on this occasion, were firefighters.

It was one of the worst experiences anyone could have with first responders. You could tell that they didn't care at all. They were hesitant to even take me out to assess me. I would have actually died if it was an actual heart issue. They treated me like I was a criminal in Hampton, VA. The lack of concern was obvious. They had this attitude and energy like I was just another poor Black person who got too high. My safety wasn't their concern at all. They even mentioned how long the night had been for them and wanted to go home, which had nothing to do with me. I have every respect for first responders, whether they are firefighters, police officers, or EMTs. I even have some friends and co-workers who are first responders, and they would have never treated anyone like that.

North Carolina, which is a part of the south and mostly a conservative state, first responders would have never treated me like that. You know, the further you go up on my side of the country, the more you get disrespected. It's not a Southern thing if you understand my twang. I'm just saying, "It's Right There!" I was so disrespected! Your feelings or personal thoughts must not be a factor when you are providing a service to protect the people. If you don't care about people, why become a firefighter or even a medic? Your whole purpose is to care about the people and save their lives. You never know who someone is or what they could be dealing with, so never prejudge and treat every patient like their well-being matters as you are supposed to. So, the ones who dealt with me at that time, listen to me as I say this. Word is bond. Time is everything. Those are keys. Grab the keys, by the door. "It's Right There!" Slam the door! You shall see me, no more. 3!

I laid off the edibles, and I started getting anxiety here and thereafter. There are some negative effects that you can have after strong doses of Weed consumption. I was prescribed some anxiety medicine after I went to a Doctor's checkup not too long after that incident. I took a few pills but didn't continue because they made me too sleepy and weren't beneficial for me in the long run. Eventually, the daily anxiety went away as I still worked out at the gym and ate well. I still smoked, but not like that. Throughout the end of 2020 and 75% through 2021, Weed was never a problem for me as I've smoked on some nights. I could take edibles again, reaching a higher consciousness without having an episode.

A lot of deep conversations and amazing creations art form wise occurred when I was under the influences. One day, while working at a Rap concert, I didn't drink enough water and overused my voice repeatedly. This caused my vocal cords to be scarred. I have been smoking Weed consecutive nights prior to this incident, and smoking dries your mouth out. The dry mouth due to Weed smoke, no water, and the overuse of the voice box were the three factors that harmed my vocal cords. I stopped smoking immediately! I knew my vocal cords were scarred by having throat problems for consecutive weeks and even a few months after this.

I've gone to different Doctors, and they didn't know the underlying issue of my throat problems. Flu-like symptoms occurred after every flareup inside the throat. I didn't have any flu's, no diseases. After finally going to an Otolaryngologist, I knew for certain I was right on the underlying issue after properly observing the inside of my throat. My vocal cords were scarred, and I had some slight acid reflux. I was prescribed a medical Steroid and Omeprazole for the acid reflux, which got more extreme after I started taking pills for that. It took so long for my vocal cords to improve; it was never the same. I was taking edibles when I had the throat flareups to heal the pain and to feel better after finally being diagnosed with gastroesophageal disease because I couldn't smoke. It completely sucked having this, and it was very uncomfortable.

It's so many foods and spices I had to avoid due to this. It took me a while to get accustomed to the disease and find that perfect balance. You should already know that I took high dosages of edibles during the time when I was completely heartbroken to cope. Never turn to any substance when you need to heal because heartbreak is the time when your mind needs to be calculated and take charge. The last time I took edibles was when I was still living with my ex-fiancé. Everything that was going on made me realize that I also needed to be completely free from that influence.

The high concentration of the edible increased the impulse of emotions significantly during my last few usages. It fed on my emotions, and I willingly let it by taking it. The feeding on emotions, especially under the influence of a substance like Weed, isn't great at all. I needed to have control of my mind every single second. I don't have to reach a higher consciousness, relieve my pain, nor go on a Spiritual journey with Weed. The only WEED I need is the one I've mentioned before. We Evolve Every Day. Manifest that WEED. That's the key, grab the key, "It's Right There!"

Personal Spirit Connection etc.

Many never knew this, but I've always had a connection with Spirits. I was able to sense their presence all the time. Unlike most people, I was never scared of a Spirit's presence, including dark ones. The goal was to understand them and get closer to them. I sensed no harm coming from them, only information. My instincts never put me in attack mode against them at all. I realized humans were more harmful to me than Spirits will ever be. I understood them and discovered I could reach them in ways an average person couldn't. Spirits guided me in many situations. I never understood why people feared or didn't want to understand them.

Films and certain Religions have brainwashed their image completely. During all my years, even while young, I was able to identify symbols and see certain wavelengths of things that a normal person shouldn't be able to see. You're probably curious to know about those things if you just read that. Even though I have told you a lot, there are certain things I must not tell you. It's very much classified, as they would say. You'll just figure it out after seeing me do historically significant things in the future. If you're reading this many years later, you'll know exactly because that future has already happened. It's there, "It's Right There!"

Since I was younger, I have been fascinated by Reptiles. These Reptile Creatures were Snakes, Dinosaurs, Alligators, etc. For some reason, they apparently just stood out to me. I understood their nature, as they appeared more interesting and eye-popping than other Creatures. There was a symbolic connection to my admiration of these Creatures. When Harry Potter spoke the Snake language in the 2nd movie, it really spoke to me. If you haven't noticed by now, I'm obviously Team Slytherin. Excuse me if you heard a little slither with my tongue. SSS!!! "It's Right There!" Cats were also creatures I admired. Cats are Ancient Creatures with powerful souls being royalty like. They have been here since the Ancient Egyptian times and will be here nearly forever. When watching the Netflix show, "Love, Death, and Robots," many stray Cats were around in the future on a human-less planet Earth filled with Robots. Cats are the perfect example of what survivors are. A powerful royal survivor is what I wanted as a pet growing up, and now I have that. Look! "It's Right There!"

As I went further in life, I was able to separate individuals by what they really are at first encounter. A person's physical appearance, the way they talk, and the power level within their soul can decide if they're a normal person or so much more. It takes plenty of practice to tell who they are, what exactly they are, and where they come from. I always knew I was so much more myself. Things I knew and could sense made me aware very early, as I mentioned already in the first part of this Chapter. Anything I saw with my eyes, whether observing Mother Nature, reading information in books, or staring at symbols, was syncing with me. I was able to know more about myself as I studied Mother Nature, people, and these symbols, including the History within them. Memories started to circulate, foreshadowing started to occur, and the ability to look at the entire world from the outside happened. I figured out so much, which includes my purpose and other's purpose inside the Multiverse.

This part is heavily connected with the Secrets of the Multiverse involving me. It's all deeper than you think. Think deeper than you could ever think when you hear the rest of this. Listen clearly as I say this. I needed to change and separate from the masses for my life to change. Everything appears so clear to me now. Capabilities are unlimited indeed, especially with the unlimited energy to absorb. There's nothing and no one that can influence me, I am complete. The goal is to be an "Unstoppable Force." That's the number one key that I teach people to be.

I've honestly been telling people who I am and what I know every day throughout my entire life in this lifetime, but many never listened nor increased the volume to the soundwaves I dished out. I once told a friend, I'll let you study me. If you look very closely 100% in real-time, even if I'm just sitting down, you'll start to notice something you've never noticed before. Once you notice that minor difference, that's when you are truly paying attention instead of distracting from seeing what's right there. I grabbed so many keys to unlock every door. To enter many realms, the gateways to open up the portals, the uncalculated level on the journey to unlimited evolution. The higher consciousness is already implanted inside of me to move forward each day. I see what I see. But do you see? If not, then maybe you need to grab the keys. That's the key, grab the key, "It's Right There!"

Secrets of the Multiverse Involving Me

You already got a head start at the end of the last Subchapter about my connection to the Secrets of the Multiverse. 1 out of 5 of this part has already been filled out for you. I had a huge admiration towards Astronomy, Ancient History, and Spirituality growing up. Many that I've come across didn't know that I've also had a secret admiration towards Psychology, the human brain. I wanted to know everything throughout every aspect of life, including people. I've questioned everything, and never just believed anything written or told to me. "I'm something of a Scientist myself," remember Green Goblin? Green has always been my favorite color. Green like money, grass, trees, and even the color that represents House Slytherin. Green! Excuse me if I slithered with my tongue. SSS!!! You could say I was like a young Lord Voldemort in a way, but not exactly, so don't get that idea. If you know, you know.

It's known that knowledge is power. I had to observe, collect information, and assess it all. Many sacrifices were made but sacrifices are necessary for human trials, even on yourself. Doing that put me in a position to see every aspect of life behind its mask, or behind its locked door as I would say. The secret is to listen and follow, but to only learn the truth and be able to no longer follow again. The key is to lead for all eternity. You could never have control of your life or do all that's possible in life if you lack information. Having information is all you need, because everything comes with it. It comes with knowing there are no limits on evolution, energy, and your capabilities. I detected all the subliminal messages throughout TV. I understood the importance of the usage of every symbol that has been displayed since the beginning of time.

I've been many things and went by many names. It all just depends on the infinite of timelines, with multiple lifetimes. I'm sort of like an Alien superstar, and there's only one of me inside this Multiverse. Unlike Kang, there are no variants. "I'm one of one, I'm number one, I'm the only one, don't even waste your time trying to compete with me." You must recognize that, even Beyonce tried to tell you, "It's Right There!"

I've been a Christian, a Buddhist, a Theist, and just a very Spiritual person with Ancient Customs who believes in deep Science in this lifetime. I realized all the Religions and Ancient Cultures practice the same things if you're looking from the outside. Power is wielded every day and fear is the ultimate power source on Earth. It keeps the flow of life and death on humans. Life, death, rebirth. 3! The most important thing I've realized, is that fear can also be used to expand life itself. That expansion can be infinite and can happen rapidly with time. Nothing that happens for you could ever be considered "bad," if there is greatness waiting for you on the other side. That's why patience and discipline with unselfishness are the crucial keys on your journey. I know 100% now, that there's never a "bad day." Every day can be great, it all just depends on how you look at it, which is perspective. It also depends on the time frame. That applies to the human term "good" and "bad" if you've been paying attention to that. You see what I did there? I told you, "It's Right There!"

A "Medium" once got on a video call with me and sensed a strong presence. He held one hand high up above his head while informing me about my presence seconds after the call started. He asked me, "You never thought about doing this yourself?" I swear this on my entire existence, and I take words like that very seriously. Word is bond, by the old order and the new. **Ordo Vetus Et Novus Ordo Mundi.** I have a witness for that encounter, for the ones who have any doubt. If you have any doubt by now, there's not much to tell you. I mean, "It's Right There." This Medium had spectacular reviews, was top notch in his field. Super skilled with his mind, heart, and soul. I chose him for a reason. I wanted "the best of the best sir," like on Men in Black. My whole goal for this call, was to get an update from an outside source other than me that knows his stuff. I needed to hear this one thing throughout this whole call.

He told me that I will get where I need to be no matter what, but the timing was up to me. I was informed that I didn't have to try hard, but just needed to be myself 100% and to be patient. It will all come when I'm ready to flip the switch, turn the knob, or turn the key. The most significant line throughout the conversation was that there was no downfall once I got where I needed to be. That line reminded me that I'm always going to do what I need to do; thinking about the future and will continue to rise. Climb! There's no downfall, if you continue to keep rising. When you're not rising, that's when things catch up to you. Up is the way to go. When you do that, there's no way they can go where you're going. You'll take off just like a rocket, and they can't stop that force. Now you see why you need WATER. You must; you Will, Accelerate The Evolution Rocket. You see, I told you, "It's Right There!" You'll travel to Venus, Mars, and across the stars to keep evolving on who you are. It will be grand, but with a slam. Grand slam! My man, I'm in grand hands. Legendary lady, don't call me crazy; "It's Right There!"

I knew it would come a time where I must take a huge leap into a role that I was always supposed to take, and I will make sure that I'm never stopped once I'm in that role. I am no longer holding back! "I am back! What it do baby!" I am skipping like Bayless, no Kawhi intended. Before I started writing this book, I planned so many things ahead. People don't even know exactly what I've been planning. "I'm planning to do all of this while you're panicking, and you're looking staring at mannequins." Chris D'Elia will even tell you, "It's Right There!" They're not paying attention at all. The thing about that is it includes them. It includes everyone! I care about every soul, but most importantly this world. Not just this world, but the whole Multiverse. I'm thinking about the Cosmos, and even outside the Cosmos.

You can't do whatever you want if life chooses you. That's an unbreakable contract for all eternity. Everything was written, pre-planned, pre-destined, or whatever you could say. Everything existed before our feelings existed. Prophecy! Purpose is everything! Without it, why are we living? Why do we deserve to have a grand life if we don't appreciate all of life and do what we must do in life? Make it grand, but with a slam. Grand slam! I have solutions for all the world's problems, and some of them will hurt some feelings. I know for certain there will be a time when people will really hate me. I'm prepared for it. I am prepared to turn all that negative energy into a positive for me. Let's go!

Oh, I forgot to tell you, you can absorb negative energy to benefit you. Dark souls aren't always what you wield or what you mostly are made of in your Multiversal code. It can be what you mostly absorb to power yourself. That's why some say, "love the haters." That significant fact about negative energy is the biggest reason why the term, "what doesn't kill you makes you stronger" exists. "Beam me up Scotty," Star Trek: Before the Mandela Effect. Attacking me will only help me. You see, I told you, "It's Right There." The world becoming a better place with mass advancement will happen regardless, it's the inevitable. The greatest gift is responsibility, and it does come with power. Responsibility also comes with a lot of fear from others, and that fear can turn into hate at a rapid rate extremely. That specific detail is why people fear having responsibilities, especially if they are all the responsibilities in the world. None of that fears me. I grew to love pressure. Pressure is when I skyrocket. All I need is WATER, Will Accelerate The Evolution Rocket. It's in my Multiversal code to take care of things.

I'm only going to make logical decisions with no bias, meaning with zero emotions involved. Fairness is fairness, and people must learn. Only the ones who serve something much bigger than themselves and truly commit, deserve everything. One of my favorite lines is from the movie "John Wick 4," and that is, "No one is excused from the consequences, not even you John Wick." He wasn't excused from the consequences no matter what, even though he constantly killed anyone who was in his way. He couldn't run forever. The hourglass became full, and his time was up. Fate caught up with John Wick. Codes exists for reasons. These laws and amendments did exist before any of our feelings existed. Prophecy! We must live by the laws we dedicate our lives to, and we must live by our codes. But not just any code, our Multiversal code.

Sometimes life chooses you; when it does, that's an unbreakable contract forever. I've said this, if you remember. You see, I told you, now say the catchphrase. You know, the Medium was actually the one who introduced me to the phrase, "Watch out!" It was very funny when he first said it, but it also foreshadowed something. Foreshadowing is all I do. I make people aware of everything, which is the reason why I wrote this book. This book is for you to be better once again and to take accountability for everything that happens to you when you ignore the consequences. So, here's my foreshadow to you. Watch out! "It's Right There!"

Chapter 11

A New You, A New World

Ureh's Mind of 3

Unlimited Capabilities, Energy, Evolution.

Mastery of Spirituality, Technology, and Time.

Earth, Universe, Multiverse

U.M.E., Mind of 3, "It's Right There!"

The Mind of 3 is another "Power of 3." It's the ultimate Power of 3. 3 is symbolic **B**iblically, **S**piritually, and **A**ncient Culturally. 3 itself is regarded as the greatest source of power throughout the Multiverse. Think of 3 as an overpowered Multiversal code implanted in all of Matter and energy. You'll have the eye to oversee everything, and it's all aligned together in strength as a gateway to open up the portals like a pyramid. 3, Eye, Pyramid. 3 Eye Pyramid! **In Hoc Secreto Credimus III.** You see, I told you, "It's Right There!" Chapter 9!

3 isn't just a number, a way of life, nor just a source of power.

3 is everything.

3 is key.

Believe in 3.

That's the key, grab the key, "It's Right There!"

Become an Unstoppable Force

Transform and become that "Unstoppable Force" that I see within you. You must see and know that you can become an "Unstoppable Force" by now. Apply all you learned from these Chapters. Learn from my mistakes and learn from yours. Learn how to identify the signs and follow them. Be as fearless as possible so that you can see the signs clearly. Being fearless will prevent you from hurting anyone you love, including yourself. The fearlessness will allow you to have no limits on your evolution, energy absorption that's beneficial for you, and neither will it limit your capabilities. You can do anything you set your mind to. All you need to do is the work. No one will do the work for you, nor will it just happen because you spoke about it. You must be willing to go hard for what you deserve. Manifestation is a process. There's a follow-up with Manifestation, like a job interview. You said all the nice things, but then you apply pressure, making sure it goes to you. You see, I told you, "It's Right There!"

Defeat fear, and don't wait until it gets ahold of you. Don't celebrate anything until the war is over. Your celebration may be delayed because there's always another war. On that note, keep fighting until nothing and no one else is standing in your way again. Let go of anything and everything that holds you back, even you. Be the main character and hero of your movie, not a side character or an extra. The different paths were written, but you can still write the script for your own story, meaning you control what type of ending you have. You are in control of your destiny! Climb a mountain and keep climbing until there are no more mountains to climb. Once you climb every mountain, build a new one yourself if you have to. The purpose of that is to never stop climbing. Never limit yourself! That's the key, grab the key, "It's Right There!"

"Life is what you make it," like Hannah Montana said, so let's make it right. Listen always! That is a skill you need to possess. The WORD is necessary if you're trying to rise above anything and anyone standing in your way. The WORD! It will always help you; you never know. Speak when you need to, don't silence yourself when it's the right time to speak up. Properly communicate, and don't be selfish with your time when it comes to communication, which includes the effort you give. Get rid of any lust you have or any lust that's trying to come your way. Swat it away like you would swat a fly. If you've been hurt, heal! Don't damage yourself more, nor hurt others. Love when you need to, and give it your all when you do, but don't let the emotions control you.

Acts of service are something both parties should demonstrate every day. Don't fear what can happen; just be ready for any result. That's why you should have high standards and make sure you can meet high standards yourself.

Don't expect a 100 if you're still a 50. You must be compatible with the person you're seeking. You will not be ready for any blessing or what's soulful for you, if you weren't ready for it. You shall receive better once you're healed, have worked on your problems, and have lifted your standards. Once you have, save yourself some time. Save yourself some time by actively placing people on a high pedestal based on what you sense from them. It's grand to do that, and here's why. Putting people on such a high pedestal will allow you to see at a very rapid rate whether people actually believe in themselves just as much as you believe in them. They either will rise or fall. Watch them rise or fall. Watch if they will doubt themselves and push away because of fear, or watch them prove that they're the person who you sense they are every time that you are there. The results are precise; it's there, "It's Right There!"

Try the One-Year Plan. This plan includes discipline and sacrifice of intimate physical touch, which is any type of sex. With this plan, you'll eliminate all the losers and will have a small pool full of winners. These winners have been looking for a person just like you. They want someone who's serious about time, love, and building a family in general. These winners will respect your sexual abstinence till marriage standard and be willing to commit to you fully. Within a year, you could be married instead of wasting years with different people or the same toxic lover. Take the One-Year Plan. Look! "It's Right There!"

Stay off social media! Pay attention to everyone and everything around you. Live more in reality. You don't need virtuality. Get to a point where you have all the necessary skills where you don't need Technology, because you become the Technology. Your mind turned into a Perfected Artificial Super Intelligence itself, and that is why you became so extremely calculated with your logic, leading you to unlimited updates. The goal is to be smart and productive even without Technology. Train your mind to be as smart as a Perfected Artificial Super Intelligence. Update yourself just like an ASI would, but to perfection. That's the key, grab the key, "It's Right There!"

Love music, but don't get hooked on it. Never let these music artists have too much influence on you, especially negatively. Don't worship them. Believe you can be great yourself. Be your own inspiration. You could be the superstar also, even maybe a bigger superstar than your favorite superstar. That's the key, grab the key, "It's Right There!"

I won't say throw away the key, but I'll say throw away the drink. Drinking won't eliminate your problems, and you can enjoy life and be a fun person without it. Throw away that drink! Protect your lungs! There's no need to smoke, and there's no need to get high when you can stay sober to reach high yourself. Every day is an opportunity to get smarter and move up in the pyramid of life, which is so high. The new WEED is so much better. You need to evolve every day. Remember, "We Evolve Every Day," and never forget it. Think about that every time you see Weed, pills, other listed drugs, a Cigarette, a Vape, or any alcoholic drink.

Addictions occur when you need to feel better. You're going to do better, then become better, and receive better because of it. Addiction-free is your future. You got to see it. I see it! How can you not see it? "It's Right There!" Trust your soul to protect you by connecting with your inner Spirit to become comfortable with other Spirits. Respect these Spirits and understand the whole Spirit Realm in general. Creatures are a part of this world, don't treat them like they're not. You could learn a few tricks yourself from these Creatures. Remember the line, "You never know who you'll meet," which applies to Entities that walk among you. Be considerate and truly watch what you say or do. Understand the ones who are very much different than you and others. On that note, figure out exactly who you are and what your purpose is. Have you wondered why you're on planet Earth? What will you be after? Who were you before? You must find out. "It's Right There."

Pay attention in school if you're still in school or planning on going back to school. Give your teacher, your loved one's teacher, or that teacher you once had some love. Forget about being cool; get smarter. Read! Read anything that can feed your brain. Read books that teach you a skill or can help improve your skills, read books that touch on the 4 main subjects, and read books about someone's life to learn from their mistakes. Be eager to learn anything, and everything! Having a student mentality in life will do you wonders. Study Astronomy, including all of Physics, while also tapping into Spirituality. Study Ancient History and learn about your country's History. Appreciate your country if you have it better than many others in other countries.

On that note, give a huge grand slam to the armed forces. Make it grand, but with a slam. Grand slam! Now give them a round of applause. Thank them for their service! These highly disciplined and skilled individuals make the ultimate sacrifices for you daily. They're the reason you can have any privilege at all and that you are safe. Their bravery shouldn't be underappreciated or swept under the rug. They deserve infinite attention and respect, the same attention and respect that people give to celebs. Appreciate all Religions for existing. If you're Religious, respect someone who believes in a different faith than you. If you're not Religious, respect anyone who's Religious and learn important things from them, even if you may never believe in their faith. Clap for the world's leaders and every individual who collaborated to serve a common purpose beneficial for the future. Without them, the world would have been in complete chaos by the people like I've said before.

Remember, don't hurt your future self. Instead of living like it's no tomorrow, live like it's a tomorrow. The more you live like it's a tomorrow, the longer you'll live. You can also have the mentality of having 24 hours to make it count. In that first 24 hours, make it count, and then consistently make it count every day. Give it all you have in this life. You can live way longer than you ever thought once you learn everything and take advantage of every single day that you breathe on planet Earth. Always do what matters so you can get ahead. That's the best way to take control of your life. Don't be consumed by TV! If you do watch TV, watch TV as educational videos, not just entertainment.

When you are no longer influenced by overwhelming emotions, you become something much bigger. Nothing and no one can divide you, not even a broadcast on your local Television. You'll get to a point where you can smile when you see how much people are emotionally driven and are controlled while you're not. Serve a higher purpose and finally become free. I promise you that once you are free, you'll refuse to ever go back. Don't ever go back, no matter what. Up is the only way to go from here on out. I would love to meet the complete version of you. You know what to do, and you understand what's required of you. In order to move to a new level, you must complete all the tasks that are required of you at your current level. Growth is defined by completion and the ability to enter new levels without fear. Complete your tasks, your tasks are there, "It's Right There!" You got the map, know all the routes, and have all the instructions to achieve anything. It's all there, it has always been there, "It's Right There."

The whole goal for this book was to even get at least 3% of the billions of people in this entire world, to look at the world from the outside. You will be able to find true peace now. A peace that you never knew existed until now. "It's Right There" isn't just a lecture of my Philosophy, isn't just a dose of Psychology, isn't just a reprogramming, isn't just a load of secret information, isn't just a Spiritual journey. It's also a campaign. "The Right Path, The Right Way." I am P.S.R. Ureh, and I approve this message. The message is there, "It's Right There!" Now, let's get to the end. Oh shit! The end! "It's Right...

The End

References

Achikeh, Cordis-Mariae, and Raphael Umeugochukwu. "The Value of Good
  Liturgical Music." UJAH: Unizik Journal of Arts and Humanities 20, no. 3
  (October 30, 2020): 133–50. https://doi.org/10.4314/ujah.v20i3.8.

Allan, Sean. "The Three Tiers of AI: Automating Tomorrow with AGI, ASI &
  ANI." Aware Group, September 4, 2018. https://www.aware.co.th/three-
  tiers-ai-automating-tomorrow-agi-asi-ani/.

Britannica. "Liturgical Music | Definition, History, Composers, & Evolution."
  Encyclopedia Britannica, 2023.
  https://www.britannica.com/topic/liturgical-music.

CERN. "The Matter-AntiMatter Asymmetry Problem | CERN." Home.cern, 2019.
  https://home.cern/science/physics/Matter-antiMatter-asymmetry-
  problem.

Colomer, Ruben. "The Three Types of Artificial Intelligence: ANI, AGI, and ASI
  — Discovering the World of AI ." Medium, April 1, 2023.
  https://medium.com/@rubencolomer/the-three-types-of-artificial-
  intelligence-ani-agi-and-asi-discovering-the-world-of-ai-36fc5fe60511.

Georgetown University. "Prescription Drugs - Health Policy Institute." Health
  Policy Institute, 2019. https://hpi.georgetown.edu/rxdrugs/.

Bible. "Bible Gateway Romans 10." web.mit.edu. Accessed December 21, 2023.
  https://web.mit.edu/jywang/www/cef/Bible/NIV/NIV_Bible/ROM+10.
  html#:~:text=That%20if%20you%20confess%20with.

New World Encyclopedia. "Gregorian Chant - New World Encyclopedia."
  www.newworldencyclopedia.org, July 14, 2017.
  https://www.newworldencyclopedia.org/entry/Gregorian_chant.

KLORIS. "Natural vs. Synthetic CBD: What's the Difference?" KLORIS,
  November 11, 2021. https://www.kloriscbd.com/blogs/cbd-
  information/natural-vs-synthetic-cbd.

Quinn, Annalisa. "The Story of Adam and Eve: From Myth to Fact and back to
  Myth Again." Washington Post, September 28, 2017, sec. Outlook.
  https://www.washingtonpost.com/outlook/the-story-of-adam-and-eve-
  from-myth-to-fact-and-back-to-myth-again/2017/09/28/a4559ea0-8cc9-
  11e7-84c0-02cc069f2c37_story.html.

Rowbury, Chris. "Choir? Chorale? Ensemble? What's in a Name?"
  https://blog.chrisrowbury.com/2014/05/choir-chorale-ensemble-whats-in-

name.html?m=1, May 26, 2014.
https://blog.chrisrowbury.com/2014/05/choir-chorale-ensemble-whats-in-name.html?m=1.

Semrush Blog. "Top 100: The Most Visited Websites in the US [2021 Top Websites Edition]." www.semrush.com, 2023. https://www.semrush.com/blog/most-visited-websites/.

Weber, Chris. "Top 10 Most Endangered Birds." Animals Around The Globe, November 29, 2021. https://www.animalsaroundtheglobe.com/most-endangered-birds/.